The Peaceful Revolution:

250 Years of Democracy in Nova Scotia

John Boileau

NIMBUS PUBLISHING

Nimbus Publishing Limited
PO Box 9166, Halifax, NS B3K 5M8
(902) 455-4286 www.nimbus.ca

Printed and bound in Canada

Author photo: Mark Doucette

Library and Archives Canada Cataloguing in Publication

Boileau, John
The peaceful revolution : 250 years of democracy
in Nova Scotia / John Boileau.

Includes index.
ISBN 978-1-55109-680-3

1. Democracy—Nova Scotia—History. 2. Representative government and representation—Nova Scotia—History. 3. Nova Scotia—Politics and government. I. Title.

JL225.B63 2008   320.4716   C2008-904312-X

We acknowledge the financial support of the Government of Canada through the Book Publishing Industry Development Program (BPIDP) and the Canada Council, and of the Province of Nova Scotia through the Department of Tourism, Culture and Heritage for our publishing activities.

Dedicated to all Nova Scotians who fought for our rights and freedoms in the long struggle for parliamentary democracy, both at home and abroad.

Many forms of government have been tried, and will be tried in this world of sin and woe. No one pretends that democracy is perfect or all-wise. Indeed, it has been said that democracy is the worst form of Government except all those other forms that have been tried from time to time.

—WINSTON CHURCHILL,
in a speech in the British House of Commons,
November 11, 1947

Contents

Foreword

By Dr. John F. Hamm, M.D. & Russell MacLellan, Q.C.
Co-chairs, Democracy 250 Organizing Committee

Between the covers of this book is a little-known story with which more people should be familiar.

John Boileau takes us on an enlightening journey from the inception of the Magna Carta, to the see-sawing battles between England and France over control of key North American footholds, to the establishment of representative and responsible governments, to today's 250th anniversary celebrations of the birth of parliamentary democracy in Canada.

In reading *The Peaceful Revolution*, one gets an appreciation of how, in the early and mid 1700s, Nova Scotia—a small, largely uninhabited peninsula on the eastern edge of what would later become Canada—caught the attention of the world's powers. Nova Scotia shaped the course of history not just in Canada, but in North American and beyond.

Readers will be introduced to a host of characters (many barely or rarely mentioned in today's history books) from Port Royal to Paris, Louisbourg to London, whose actions and influence brought our small province both great pride and great shame.

The Peaceful Revolution is honest history, openly acknowledging that not everything in Nova Scotia's past is worthy of celebration. It tells the story of how the ancestors of today's Mi'kmaq were almost wiped out by the new diseases their overseas guests brought with them, and by British colonial governors who sought to rid their newly adopted land of "the savages."

Le Grand Dérangement, the Expulsion of the Acadians, was another sad chapter in Nova Scotia's history, as the British forced hundreds of French families from the lands they fished and farmed to settle in far-off places, many never to return.

Despite the injustices of the colonial authorities of the past, Nova Scotians can take pride in many of their predecessors' achievements. Nova Scotia laid the foundation upon which all governments in Canada, and many beyond, built the institutions that guarantee our many rights and freedoms today. It was in Nova Scotia that the first Supreme Court in North America convened, the first elected assembly met, responsible government was born, and a highly principled man by the name of Joseph Howe stood alone to defend freedom of speech and freedom of the press.

In this special year of celebration, marking the 250th anniversary of representative government in Nova Scotia and the birth of parliamentary democracy in Canada, Democracy 250 is pleased to join John Boileau and Nimbus Publishing in shining the spotlight on Nova Scotia and its enormously important history.

The Peaceful Revolution is perhaps the most complete version of Nova Scotia's long, sometimes painful, but ultimately proud and peaceful journey towards democracy. A truthful story, replete with the good and the bad, it fills the gaps other historical accounts leave empty. We hope that, 250 years after Nova Scotia introduced Canada to parliamentary democracy, *The Peaceful Revolution* also reminds its readers of the importance of democracy and the power of every vote.

PREFACE

OST CITIZENS OF NOVA SCOTIA—AND CANADA— seem to take the benefits and privileges of democracy for granted. Perhaps they do not fully realize the very lengthy amount of time and very great number of people involved in achieving it. Nova Scotia played a key role in the long struggle for parliamentary democracy in Canada, as well as for some of the fundamental freedoms we enjoy today. It was in this tiny province, then a British colony, that representative government first appeared in Canada, some 250 years ago in 1758.

Under representative government, certain people have the right to choose, through elections, some of their fellow citizens to represent them in a gathering or assembly. Once constituted, this assembly then has the authority—in concert with other branches of the government—to govern the people through enacting laws and other regulations.

Ninety years later, in 1848, responsible government also debuted in Nova Scotia. Between these two seminal events, freedom of the press and freedom of speech were achieved for the first time in Canada by Joseph Howe in Nova Scotia. Shortly afterwards, Howe became the key player in the struggle for responsible government. Under responsible government, government ministers—known collectively as a cabinet—are chosen by the party that has a majority of members in the assembly. These ministers are responsible, or accountable, to this majority, and can be forced to resign if they lose its confidence.

The achievement of these fundamental democratic milestones is a remarkable story that deserves to be told to a wide audience. The purpose of this book is to tell this story, and the 250th anniversary of representative government provides a fitting opportunity.

In writing this story for modern readers, I felt it was important not only to describe the emergence of representative democracy in Nova Scotia 250 years ago, but to properly place it in the context of the wider story of the beginnings of parliamentary democracy—the Magna Carta of 1215—and the early history of this province. While the establishment of representative government was a key milestone, it is not the end of the story. I felt it was equally important to continue the account of the progress of democracy with the efforts of those involved in the much longer struggle for the achievement of responsible democracy in 1848, along the way attaining freedom of the press and freedom of speech. To complete the story, I have included other advances in the democratic process that followed later, bringing events forward to our time.

Governments—both the type of government and the people who comprise them—have changed throughout history on an irregular, yet surprisingly frequent, basis. War, conquest, rebellion, revolution, assassination, and coup d'état are some of the more spectacular— and usually speedy—ways that one group or individual in power has replaced another group or individual. World history is replete with well-known stories from centuries of warfare: the conquests of European empires; the British, French, American, Russian, Chinese, and other revolutions, rebellions, and civil wars; the killing of national leaders; and a plethora of modern-age coups, the latter particularly in the underdeveloped regions of the globe. Nova Scotia has had more than its fair share of changes in government through warfare and imperial conquests, as described in this book. For example, the control of Port Royal changed nine or ten times throughout its history, with Mi'kmaq, French, Scottish, Acadians, English, New Englanders, and even the Dutch in charge during various periods.

But governments have also changed in much more peaceful—and usually more protracted—ways. Nova Scotia was a key player in such events. The general advance of democracy, in particular the tradition of parliamentary democracy that defines Canada today, took centuries to achieve. Although parliamentary democracy as we now know it began in Britain, its introduction to Canada occurred in Nova Scotia in the form of two important achievements—representative government, followed later by responsible government.

Nova Scotia has a long and colourful history. Originally occupied by the Paleo-Indian ancestors of today's Mi'kmaq about thirteen thousand years ago, it was "discovered" by European fishermen sometime before 1500 A.D. Permanent European settlement began in 1604, followed the next year by the founding of Port Royal by the Frenchman Sieur de Monts and his navigator and cartographer, Samuel de Champlain. It thus became the oldest continuously inhabited European settlement in America north of the Spanish possessions in Florida. Because both the British and French claimed this territory (the English assertion was based on John Cabot's alleged landfall on Cape Breton Island during his 1497 voyage), it soon became an area hotly contested by both nations.

Over the next century and a half, the possession of Acadia, as the French called it, passed between French and English hands on several occasions, with both countries occasionally occupying different parts of it at the same time. Mainland Nova Scotia definitively became British with the Treaty of Utrecht in 1713, but Cape Breton Island and Prince Edward Island remained French. Finally, the Treaty of Paris, which ended the Seven Years' War in 1763, ceded all of France's possessions in North America, less two tiny islands off the coast of Newfoundland, to the British.

Once Britain took possession of these former French lands, it had to govern them. The progress of government in Nova Scotia occurred over a long period of time. It developed partly by acts of the Crown—which were proclaimed by the king and his ministers in London, or by the governor and executive council in Annapolis Royal (later in

Halifax)—and partly by the actions of the colonial assembly, once it was established. The actions of these groups modified existing institutions and created new ones appropriate for a colony that had expanded beyond its original roots. Along with these developments, relationships were continuously changing between the governor, executive council, and legislative assembly.

Some of the most well-known figures in provincial, national, and even world history played their part in one way or another in Nova Scotia's lengthy struggle for parliamentary democracy. Many others remain if not nameless at least faceless to modern citizens. They are the ordinary men—and women, in more recent times—who fought for one of the most basic rights that democracy bestows upon individuals: choosing others to represent them in deciding how they are to be governed.

The story of how the small, isolated, and relatively unimportant colony of Nova Scotia was the first to achieve two of the major developments in parliamentary democracy in Canada—representative government and responsible government—as well as freedom of the press and freedom of speech, is one of which every Nova Scotian and Canadian should be aware—and proud.

I was particularly delighted to undertake this task for Nimbus, as my roots go deep into Nova Scotia's history. On my Acadian side—my father's mother—our family genealogy notes that Pierre Lejeune (my great-great-great-great-great-great-great-great-great-grandfather), who was born in the village of Martaizé in the French province of Poitou in 1595, came to Acadia between 1618 and 1620 as a single man. He was an *engagé*, a contract labourer hired for a specific period of time, and worked for Charles de Biencourt's fur trading operation, probably as a clerk. In 1621—the year after the Pilgrims stepped ashore from the *Mayflower* at Plymouth Rock and the same year that Sir William Alexander received the grant of Nova Scotia from King James I of England—he took as his wife an unnamed "Indienne Mic-Mac."

Pierre became one of the founding generation of Acadians. Catherine, the daughter of Pierre and his Mi'kmaq bride, was born in 1633 at Cape Sable and married François Savoie at Port Royal around 1651. Over the years the line is traced through the Chiasson, Forest, Bourque, and Bourgeois families, the latter the maiden name of my paternal grandmother, Rachael. This direct link to the aboriginal and European beginnings of this province is a connection of which I am very proud.

I would like to thank Dan Soucoup and Sandra McIntyre at Nimbus for asking me to write this book to coincide with the province of Nova Scotia's commemorations of the 250th anniversary of representative government. Sandra has since moved to—if not greener, at least other—pastures in Calgary; I will miss her valuable counsel greatly. The other members of the wonderful team at Nimbus, including Patrick Murphy and Penelope Jackson, editors; Heather Bryan, production manager; Terrilee Bulger, sales manager; and Diane Faulkner, marketing coordinator, have once again given me the same great assistance that they have in the past. In particular, I must single out Penelope for the quality of her editing. She has done a tremendous job in making my words read so much better.

Locally, the members of the provincial Democracy 250 Organizing Committee have been very helpful. In particular, I would like to thank co-chairmen and former premiers John Hamm and Russell MacLellan for writing the foreword. Additionally, I must single out Moira MacLeod, director of communications for the Democracy 250 secretariat, who has promptly provided the answers to my many questions, as well as other assistance.

Other honourable mentions for assistance go to Jeanne Howell at the Cambridge Military Library; Stephen Kimber of the School of Journalism at the University of King's College; Carla Kempt at the Executive Council Office of Nova Scotia; Margaret Murphy and Heather Ludlow at the Legislative Library; Shirley Robb, Catherine

Neily, Paul Chenard, and Alison Beckett at Communications Nova Scotia; Gary Shutlak, Philip Hartling, Anjali Vohra, Gail Judge, Barry Smith, and George Dupuis at Nova Scotia Archives and Records Management; and A. J. B. (John) Johnston at Parks Canada. And, as always, thanks to Miriam, who let me get on with my writing, even when there were lawns to cut, gardens to weed, trees to prune, decks to paint, and snow to shovel.

I am also indebted to several earlier writers and researchers who have delved into and written about the development of the democratic process in the wider context of government and politics. I could not have completed this book without their invaluable efforts. Despite their fine work, any errors of fact or interpretation are strictly my own.

JOHN BOILEAU
'Lindisfarne'
Glen Margaret, Nova Scotia
May 20, 2008
250th anniversary of the proclamation calling for the election of the first general assembly for Nova Scotia, the first body of elected representatives of the people in Canada

Prologue
The Beginnings of Parliamentary Democracy

1215
Magna Carta
issued

1258
Provisions of
Oxford issued

The Great Charter

IT IS A COMMON MISCONCEPTION—ARTFULLY promoted by the fertile imaginations of historical novelists and Hollywood screenwriters—that medieval English kings were absolute monarchs, holding the power of life and death over all their subjects. While this may have been true for the majority of a king's people, there was a distinct group over whom the sovereign exercised his rule but lightly: his earls and barons.

As several English monarchs learned repeatedly throughout their reigns, there were limits to the exercise of autocratic rule—and to the patience of their nobles. The relationship between a king and his barons was not the same as the relationship between king and commoner or between baron and serf. The reason for this difference was the decentralized nature of feudal society.

In the feudal system, no ruler had enough men, money, or *matériel* under his direct control to be able to totally disregard the wishes of his most powerful barons. To rule, a king needed to persuade the great council, which was made up of the country's great men—its leading barons and bishops—to do things his way. To be persuasive, a king needed to be respected, resolute, realistic, and reasonable. If he wasn't, then the barons took action to curb the king's power. An early instance of the imposition of

Contemporary painting of King John

Knights in battle during the reign of King John

limits on the powers of a king led to one of the keystone documents in human history—the Magna Carta, or Great Charter—one of the earliest records devoted to the rule of law and good governance.

By all accounts, King John, who ruled from 1199 to 1216, was not a very nice person. He more than lived up to his various villainous portrayals as the mythical Robin Hood's archenemy and became one of the most unpopular monarchs in English history—for which he alone must bear the main responsibility. John secretly betrayed his father, Henry II, in his dying days; schemed to overthrow his brother, Richard I (nicknamed the Lionheart), while the latter was away on crusade; had his marriage annulled so he could marry another woman whose estates would improve his kingdom; lost Normandy and Anjou in France to the English Crown; imposed additional heavy taxes; and clashed with the Pope, which led to his excommunication—an extremely severe penalty in the Middle Ages.

John's heavy-handed ways perverted good governance and alienated his barons. The last straw came when John's efforts to recapture his lost French territories failed in July 1214. Rebellion followed. When the capital city of London went over to the rebels in May 1215, John's only practical option was to make peace. Subsequently, the barons met and agreed that they would force the king to accept a declaration of the principles of government and of the proper relationship between a king and his feudal nobles. In a pleasant sunlit meadow at Runnymede, near Windsor, on the south bank of the River Thames, John met with a delegation of his barons on June 15, 1215, and affixed his seal to the Magna Carta. The Great Charter ensured feudal rights and restated English law. It is the most important constitutional document in English history.

Simon de Montfort

John's son, who ruled as Henry III from 1216 to 1272, was England's first minor ruler. When he came of age, Henry relied on French favourites to help him govern the country and ignored the barons who had a feudal right to advise him. As the dissatisfaction of the English nobles grew over this arrangement—which they perceived as an insult to their ancient rights—they came to realize they would have to take action to regain their proper role in governing the country. In 1258, the barons persuaded Henry to agree to a parliament and to a joint baronial council—twelve chosen by the king and twelve by dissident nobles—that would recommend measures for the reform of the country. Simon de Montfort was one of the important opposition barons.

→

King John repudiated the Magna Carta within the year, claiming that, as his assent had been forced, he was not bound by his oath. This action led to a baronial revolt—in effect, a civil war—during which John died, effectively removing the cause of the rebellion. John's son and other successor English monarchs reissued the Magna Carta, establishing it as a part of the permanent law of the land—and as precedent. In England, because custom and tradition are held in such high esteem, to quote historical precedent is the best way to support a claim.

Although some of John's successors tried to ignore the law and repeated his abuses and those of his predecessors—abuses they had promised to reform—over time the rule of law prevailed. The Magna Carta remains the fundamental precedent, a source of basic principles and the first great charter of the Western world.

The twenty-four barons drew up the Provisions of Oxford, a series of revolutionary articles that committed Henry to a plan of reform and gave the council supervisory control of the government. It was also agreed that Parliament, which had previously been irregular gatherings of the civil and clerical lords and the king's legal advisors, would meet three times a year.

Had they been followed, the Provisions of Oxford would have made the king a constitutional monarch. Unfortunately, Henry inherited some of his father's deceitfulness and succeeded in rallying enough support to repudiate his acceptance of the council of barons within two years—at the same time promising reforms. Without a strong leader, the resolve of the barons crumbled. Henry's promises bought him time, but eventually his insincerity was obvious. Then the strongman the barons needed stepped to the fore.

When Henry reneged on his word, Simon de Montfort led the barons in a revolt against the king that ended with Henry's capture at

A 1965 American postage stamp commemorating the 750th anniversary of the Magna Carta

the Battle of Lewes in 1264. De Montfort then became the de facto ruler of England, governing by military dictatorship, although he still considered himself a loyal subject of Henry. De Montfort's genius—and not all historians agree on his motives—was to realize that to achieve reform he needed a broader base of support than just a few barons. In March 1265, he called together a parliament in Westminster Hall. It was composed not only of the nobility, but also of two knights from each shire and two to four "good and loyal men" from each city and borough.

The name and idea of a parliament was not new: it was the term used to describe the king meeting with his advisors to discuss matters of state. The term came from the Old French *parlement*, for "discussion." Even the concept of representation was not new: juries had been selected for some time to act for their neighbours. What was unique was the meeting of feudal advisers and elected representatives in one national assembly, coming together to discuss the government and the laws of the land.

Historians consider this the first true Parliament, the beginnings of the British House of Commons and the start of parliamentary democracy. Unfortunately, this first true Parliament was short-lived and de Montfort's army was defeated by royalist followers of

SIMON DE MONTFORT

Simon de Montfort (c.1208–65) was French by birth and education, but went to England in 1230 to revive his family's claim to the earldom of Leicester, in which he was successful. Initially a friend of Henry—in 1238 he married the king's sister Eleanor—de Montfort eventually came to believe that Henry was unfit to rule and was one of the leading barons who forced the Provisions of Oxford on the king.

After de Montfort's death, Henry confiscated the lands of de Montfort's supporters, who fought back from their forest and fen hideouts. Known as "the Disinherited," the original Robin Hood legend may be based on one of them. This blurs somewhat the popular modern belief (fabricated in the eighteenth century) of Robin Hood fighting against Henry's father, John, when John tried to seize control of England while his brother, Richard I, was involved in the crusade to recover Jerusalem from the Moslems.

A set of 1965 British postage stamps commemorating Simon de Montfort and the 700th anniversary of Parliament

Henry's son, Edward, at Evesham that August, in a battle in which de Montfort was decapitated.

De Montfort was dead, but the concept of the national representative body he conceived lived on. During the remaining seven years of his reign, Henry III frequently convened Parliament, although it was not yet the legislative gathering it was to become. The king could still pronounce laws or statutes on his own initiative. But the seed of a representative Parliament had been firmly planted, to grow and develop into a strong and healthy tree of democracy over the next few centuries— thanks to Simon de Montfort's vision.

Chapter 1
Conflict for a Continent

Mi'kma'ki

THE PALEO-INDIAN ANCESTORS OF NOVA SCOTIA'S Mi'kmaq—known as the Maritime Archaic culture—probably reached the Maritimes around 11,000 B.C. and quickly adapted to their surroundings. They became extremely adept at utilizing the bounty that nature provided them. They hunted, fished, and gathered, travelling in small bands with the seasons between the interior and the coast. Although the forest provided some of their food, they were primarily dependent on coastal mammals, fish, birds, and shellfish, which provided ninety percent of their diet.

When harsh winter winds lashed the seacoasts, they retreated deep into the forest to hunt beaver, moose, and caribou, and remained there until the spring. For some as yet unknown reason, the Paleo-Indian presence in Nova Scotia seems to disappear from the archaeological record for about eight thousand years, to be replaced eventually by the Mi'kmaq.

The traditional lands of the Mi'kmaq—known as Mi'kma'ki—were all of Nova Scotia, Prince Edward Island, and coastal New

A Mi'kmaq family with sleigh and snowshoes

Brunswick up into the Gaspé Peninsula, an area of more than 130,000 square kilometres. Mi'kmaq oral history states that this territory consisted of seven districts, each with a descriptive name based on a defining characteristic of that area.

Mi'kmaq Political Structure

Based on the small population and the self-sufficiency of each family unit of traditional Mi'kmaq, social anthropologist Harald Prins—who lived among the Maine Mi'kmaq for ten years—considers that "traditional Mi'kmaq political patterns included a loosely structured social organization, participatory decision making, voluntary association, minimalized institutionalization, and situational (as-needed) political leadership based on consensus instead of coercion," which made a "highly egalitarian society."

The Mi'kmaq territory was overseen by a *kji'saqmaw* or grand chief—a "first among equals"—with the district chiefs under him, of which he was one. It is highly likely that the *kji'saqmaw*'s function was largely ceremonial. Each district, which contained a number of bands or extended kin-groups, also had a council. Each kin-group was led by a headman, known as a *saqmaw*, a term used to denote respect for a leader who commanded other men.

Bands ranged in size from fewer than thirty to more than three hundred and were highly fluid, loosely organized communities. Based on the voluntary nature of the bands, their size fluctuated from year to year. *Saqmaws* usually came from distinguished families that had

A view of the interior of a wigwam

produced respected leaders for generations and normally held the title for life, although the designation was not strictly hereditary.

Saqmaws met periodically as required at band and regional levels to discuss internal and external affairs. Among the most important duties were the allocation of hunting territory and the settlement of disputes. The *saqmaws'* followers had a large degree of autonomy and the chiefs did not use any form of coercive control over them. Instead, the *saqmaws'* leadership was based on persuasion, example, custom, and ties of kinship or alliance, but obedience was never compulsory. Such vague authority was a concept unknown to Europeans, and it baffled them. A society less structured and authoritarian than their own was inevitably regarded as primitive.

The Europeans Arrive

Today, it is hard to imagine just how immense and empty of people the North American wilderness was four hundred years ago. The continent's aboriginal population at the time of European contact has

A Mi'kmaq girl of Nova Scotia

been variously estimated at anywhere from two to eighteen million people, with seven million nearest to a generally accepted figure. The Mi'kmaq may have numbered as many as thirty-five thousand, although fifteen thousand may be a more reasonable estimate.

Although the exact date of the earliest contact between native North Americans and Europeans is impossible to state, among the first meetings were those involving the Mi'kmaq. The traditional lands of the Mi'kmaq were the section of the New World closest to the Old and among the first the Europeans reached. As a result, the Mi'kmaq and other Atlantic coast tribes bore the brunt of first contact.

Prior to contact with the white man, the Mi'kmaq thought they were the easternmost people in the world. Perhaps as early as the mid-1400s each group was aware of the other's existence. Some of the initial contacts with Europeans—whom the Mi'kmaq called *wenju* ("stranger")—are shrouded in controversy and myth.

By the 1500s, contact became more frequent as Europeans returned to the New World for cod and whales. Drying their catch onshore took time, during which they had to maintain good relations with the natives, who wanted to trade furs and fresh meat for European goods. The Europeans' interest in fish soon turned to fur, especially beaver. The fishermen found a ready market at home for these furs and made a handsome profit. The fur trade had begun.

Then, in 1604, Pierre du Gua de Monts, Jean de Poutrincourt et de Saint-Juste, Samuel de Champlain, and their companions became part of a chain of events that would eventually see the European settlement of the vast North American land mass. It changed the world—and the native peoples who lived there—forever. The next year, the tiny outpost at Port Royal became the first successful and sustained settlement.

The Founding of Acadia

In the words of noted New Brunswick scholar Dr. William Ganong, the action of this small group of Frenchmen "stands as a milestone on the world's road of progress." In 1603, the French king appointed Sieur de Monts as lieu-

Champlain superintending the building of the Port Royal habitation

tenant general of Acadia, at the time a vast territory stretching from present-day Philadelphia north to Cape Breton Island, up the Saint Lawrence River past Sorel and as far inland as de Monts could travel. In return for a ten-year monopoly on the lucrative fur trade, de Monts agreed to settle the country with sixty (reduced from one hundred) colonists each year and convert the aboriginals to Catholicism.

The little expedition, under the command of de Monts and with Champlain as cartographer, departed Le Havre in two small ships with 120 souls on board in March 1604. De Monts chose a small island in a river on today's international boundary between Canada and the United States as a suitable place for a permanent settlement and named it the island of Sainte-Croix. The men constructed dwellings and put the island in a state of defence in a very short time. In August de Monts sent the ships back to France with a third of the company. For those left behind, the first winter was a dreadful experience. Of the seventy-nine who remained, thirty-five died and more than twenty "were very near it," mostly due to scurvy.

The experience had a sobering effect on the French and in June de Monts decided to go in search of a more suitable site for a settlement, one with a milder climate. With time short to build houses, they sailed across the Bay of Fundy to Port Royal after dismantling most of their buildings, and reconstructed them on a sheltered site. So ended the disastrous first year of the French in Acadia. After moving to Port Royal, the colony recovered, grew slowly, and then flourished—the beginning of the permanent European settlement of Canada. But the ascent of the Europeans meant the descent of the native peoples, a headlong plunge into a downward spiral from which they never recovered.

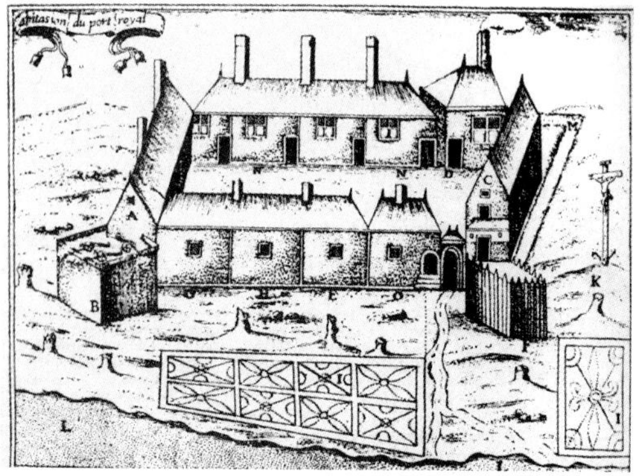
Champlain's sketch of the habitation at Port Royal

European Impact

It was the establishment of Port Royal and other permanent communities that had by far the greatest—and the worst—impact upon the natives. The introduction of European tools, weapons, clothes, and foods drastically altered the aboriginal lifestyle. While this initially seemed to improve their quality of life, it was only temporary, and the natives quickly became dependent on imported goods that they could not duplicate. As well, soon after the French arrived, the Mi'kmaq began trapping fur-bearing animals for trade, instead of hunting and travelling to their traditional fishing and food-gathering sites. They became so dependent on European trade goods that trapping became their new way of life. The whole pattern of their subsistence cycle was altered.

Common European diseases to which the Mi'kmaq had never before been exposed devastated large segments of the native population whenever they struck—and they struck repeatedly—inflicting losses of up to seventy-five percent. Additionally, eating more European foods weakened their resistance to common diseases they could have shrugged off earlier. These European influences reshaped aboriginal culture in a surprisingly short time and a way of life that had existed virtually unaltered for thousands of years was changed forever.

The Struggle for Supremacy

Struggles between France and Britain for supremacy in Europe soon blossomed into conflict abroad. Once explorers moved into new territories, traders and merchants quickly followed them, intent on being the first to discover the riches the new lands possessed—fish and furs, gold and gems, silks and spices—and being the first to exploit them. Little thought was given to governance of the new lands until colonists arrived. France and England clashed in India, the West Indies, Africa, and elsewhere. But nowhere was the struggle greater— or with greater ramifications—than in North America. The tiny French outpost at Port Royal did not escape the larger conflict being waged on a broader front.

The courtyard of the Port Royal habitation

The Port Royal habitation

De Monts returned to France and remained there to try and prevent rival merchants from having his monopoly revoked. In 1606, he put Poutrincourt in charge at Port Royal. Poutrincourt brought with him his son, Charles de Biencourt, his cousin, Claude de Saint-Etienne de La Tour, and Claude's son, Charles. De Monts ultimately lost his ten-year monopoly when King Henri IV of France unexpectedly revoked it in 1607, forcing the colonists to abandon Port Royal. Poutrincourt returned three years later, in 1610, having obtained de Monts' seigneur-

Sieur de Monts

ial grant of the immediate area around Port Royal. The local Mi'kmaq, who had maintained the fort in good order during the absence of the French, were delighted. Meanwhile, south of Acadia the English had entered the scene.

The British colonies along the Atlantic seaboard considered present-day Maine to be part of their territory and were not willing to tolerate French encroachments into the area. In October 1613, Virginian adventurer Captain Samuel Argall sailed into Annapolis Basin and put Port Royal to the torch while the settlers were absent in the fields and forests. His raid marked the beginning of a 150-year rivalry between France and England for control of the region. Argall sailed away two weeks later, leaving many settlers to die of starvation that winter. Most of those who survived did so because of the kindness of the Mi'kmaq.

Poutrincourt deeded his seigneury to his son, Biencourt, who had stayed on at Port Royal with the La Tours. Around 1617–18, Biencourt moved his base from Port Royal to Cape Sable, while Charles de La Tour operated out of present-day Maine. When Biencourt died in 1623, he left his rights to Acadia to his brother, who remained in France, but left the running of the colony to Charles de La Tour. La Tour then built a fort at Cape Sable, the only French presence left in Acadia. As the weakened colony struggled over the next few years, events in Britain took a turn that produced a temporary change in government and a lasting effect on Acadia.

The burning of Port Royal in 1613 by Captain Samuel Argall

The First Nova Scotian

One of the courtiers at the court of King James VI of Scotland—who was also James I of England—was Sir William Alexander (c. 1577–1640), later Earl of Stirling. Alexander was a cultured individual, a scholar, poet, and translator of the Book of Psalms (it was James who ordered a new translation of the Bible, which became known as the Authorized Version or King James's Bible). James made Alexander a member of the Scottish Privy Council in 1615, where the latter quickly gained the king's confidence.

Alexander persuaded the king to let him found a New Scotland. After all, there was a New England, a New France, and a New Spain, so why not a New Scotland as a sign of Scotland's importance and to reflect Scottish glory? Alexander already had experience in colonization; he

William Alexander, Earl of Stirling and Viscount Canada, gave Nova Scotia its name and symbols

The armorial bearings of Sir William Alexander

had established the Ulster plantation in Northern Ireland.

In 1621, James granted Alexander the whole territory comprising today's Maritime provinces and Quebec's Gaspé Peninsula. James's claim to this huge territory was based on John Cabot's voyages of 1497–98—the first recorded landfalls on the North American continent since the Norsemen—when he claimed the area for Henry VII of England. It didn't seem to concern either James or Alexander that New Scotland already a name—Acadia—and was occupied by another nation—France.

To raise money for his colonization project, James authorized Alexander to create knight-baronetcies (the lowest level of the hereditary peerage), which he then sold to raise money for the project. Purchasers of these baronetcies agreed to fulfill several conditions for settlement of the new colony, but few of them followed through on their promises. None of them ever went to New Scotland.

Alexander never visited the colony himself, either, but sent his son, Sir William Alexander the Younger. The son led an attempt at colonization in 1629 at the still-abandoned Port Royal with about seventy colonists. Through a quirk of fate, among the colonists was Claude de La Tour, captured by the British on a ship off the coast of Gaspé in 1627. La Tour was taken to England, where he befriended Alexander through his charm. Claude became a baronet of Nova Scotia, apparently in exchange for promising he could convince his son Charles—who occupied a fort at Cape Sable—to come over to the English side.

But Charles was made of stronger stuff than his father, and refused to betray his king when Claude arrived off Cape Sable in the summer of 1630 with additional Scottish colonists and two warships. Claude was dumbfounded—France had virtually neglected Acadia and the baronetcies allocated them a huge amount of territory. Infuriated, Claude attacked his son's fort. Two days later, he withdrew to Port Royal after Charles successfully held out against him.

Meanwhile, things were not going well for the Scots at Port Royal. Thirty had died during their first winter and their patron, James I, was dead as well. His successor, Charles I, returned Acadia to France, and ordered Alexander to withdraw his colonists and destroy everything they had built. Although Alexander's dream of New Scotland came to naught, he did provide a lasting legacy to the province, in its name, coat of arms, and other symbols. As well, about a

NOVA SCOTIA SYMBOLS

Name: Sir William Alexander named his colony New Scotland, but used its Latin form—Nova Scotia. Although *Nova Scotia* is a Latin term, both the federal and provincial governments unnecessarily translate it into French as *Nouvelle-Écosse.*

Coat of Arms: King Charles I granted a coat of arms to the Royal Province of Nova Scotia in 1625, the oldest arms of all the overseas Commonwealth colonies. The complete armorial achievement consists of the shield of arms, surmounted by a royal helmet with a blue and silver rolled ribbon representing the royal cloak. Above the helmet are heraldic symbols—two joined hands, one mailed and the other bare, supporting a spray of laurel representing peace and a thistle representing Scotland. On the

→

left is a royal unicorn and on the right a seventeenth-century representation of a native. At the base the mayflower is entwined with a Scottish thistle, which was added in 1929. Above all is the motto "Munit Hæc et Altera Vincit" ("One Defends and the Other Conquers").

Shield of Arms: A white or silver cross on a field of blue is the national arms of Scotland. Nova Scotia's is the same, but with the colours reversed. At the centre a smaller shield of royal arms contains the royal lion within a double red border on a field of yellow or gold. When King Charles granted these arms in 1625 it was considered a mark of royal favour.

Flag: The flag consists of the royal arms superimposed on a blue Cross of Saint Andrew with a white background. It was the first flag in the Commonwealth outside of Britain to be authorized by Royal Charter.

hundred baronets of Nova Scotia are still in existence today as peers of the realm.

The Great Rivalry

In 1627, the king of France granted all of Canada and Acadia to the Company of New France as feudal territory. In turn, in 1632 the company granted several large seigneuries in Acadia to Isaac de Razilly, who was also lieutenant general for New France and governor of Acadia. Meanwhile, in the summer of 1631, Charles de La Tour finally received the word for which he long been waiting. Louis XIII put him in charge of Acadia and appointed him as his lieutenant general for the colony. The next year, the Treaty of Saint-Germain-en-Laye, signed in March 1632, gave Acadia, as well as New France, back to the French.

In September, Razilly and three hundred colonists arrived in Acadia and established Fort Sainte-Marie-de-Grâce at the mouth of the LaHave River, not far from present-day Bridgewater. It was the first serious attempt by the French to actually settle the colony rather than exploit it for its riches. Razilly was La Tour's superior, and established his capital at his new fort, rather than at its traditional location, Port Royal.

La Tour and Razilly soon worked out an agreement to share in the fur trade, with La Tour operating from Cape Sable and the mouth of the Saint John River. Relations were amicable enough between the two men, but Razilly died in 1636, and matters took a turn for the worse when Razilly's brother, Claude, put the aristocratic Charles Menou d'Aulnay in charge of one of the fur-trading companies. D'Aulnay regarded La Tour as a low-born individual, unfit to be lieutenant general for Acadia. The rivalry between the two men worsened, compounded by a serious error on the part of French authorities in 1638.

Marie de La Tour defending Fort Saint John against Charles Menon d'Aulnay

In an attempt to calm the tensions between La Tour and d'Aulnay, French officials split control of Acadia between the two. They gave d'Aulnay present-day New Brunswick, but not La Tour's fort at the mouth of the Saint John River. La Tour received peninsular Nova Scotia, but not Port Royal. It was a recipe for disaster. Fortunately, d'Aulnay had already started to move settlers from Sainte-Marie-de-Grâce to Port Royal, to make it Acadia's capital once more. That same year, Louis XIII abruptly named d'Aulnay as the new lieutenant general for Acadia, another blow to La

Marie de La Tour died after she surrendered her husband's fort

Tour. Open warfare broke out between the two men, which lasted for several years and led to numerous deaths on both sides.

The rivalry came to a head in February 1645, when d'Aulnay attacked La Tour's fort with two hundred men while it was being defended by

Marie de La Tour and a mere forty-five men during her husband's absence. Marie gallantly held out for three days before surrendering, after d'Aulnay promised to spare her men. D'Aulnay reneged on his word and ordered the execution of all of La Tour's men save one, who acted as hangman. He forced Marie to watch the executions, a rope around her own neck. She died three weeks later, possibly of sorrow, rage, or poison.

After d'Aulnay drowned in 1650, La Tour returned to France and begged for an inquiry into the events in Acadia. It found d'Aulnay responsible for the bloodshed in Acadia and returned the governor's appointment to La Tour. He sailed back to Acadia in 1653 with several colonists, occupied Port Royal, and—in a strange twist of fate—married d'Aulnay's widow, Jeanne Motin. By then, there were more than four hundred European settlers in the region, the basis for the development of the Acadian people.

Chapter 2
Colonial Government in Acadia

French Feudalism

USING A LEGAL FICTION KNOWN AS THE Doctrine of First Discovery, the French declared that the Crown possessed sovereign title over the vast area called New France. It didn't matter to them that the Mi'kmaq and other tribes had lived there for thousands of years. Because the indigenous peoples were non-Christians, the French did not accept the idea of aboriginal land title. As a result, the French never bothered to sign treaties with the native peoples; after all, if the aboriginals didn't own the land in the first place, they couldn't sign it over.

Once the French decided they owned the land, they exported their feudalistic form of government—essentially the fiefdoms of the Middle Ages—to Acadia. The king distributed large pieces of territory to individuals or companies, who were required to improve their holdings at their expense. Such individuals were called seigneurs, and the lands they held were known as seigneuries. Seigneurs in turn allocated their grants to the colonists they brought out to settle the country. The seigneur was a feudal lord and as such exercised considerable control over his people. He provided protection and dispensed justice, and in return his tenants owed him feudal dues, labour, military service—and deference. Seigneurs also had several obligations to the king,

1713
Treaty of Utrecht gives mainland Nova Scotia to Britain

1720
Governor Philipps establishes executive council at Annapolis Royal

1745
Louisbourg falls to New Englanders

FRANCE IN NORTH AMERICA

Although French explorers were among the earliest to visit the New World, they were not the first; they followed English, Spanish, and Portuguese ones. Beginning with the first voyage of Jacques Cartier in 1534, when he planted a cross on the shores of the Gaspé and claimed the territory for France, the French government sponsored successive expeditions across the Atlantic Ocean. Initially, the French were searching for a new—and shorter—route to the Orient, where they hoped to exploit its fabled riches. It took a few years before the explorers realized that North America was a continent and not some part of the Far East. Even then, the search for an expected Northwest Passage through or around North America to the Orient continued.

Although France had other colonies in the New World, in the Caribbean area, the French concentrated their efforts on North America, and from the early sixteenth century developed into one of its principal colonizers. The northern part of French

An Acadian habitant's home

and if they weren't met, their land grants could be revoked.

This political system had a tremendous impact on the Mi'kmaq. It redefined their territorial arrangements, focused their economic activities, influenced their seasonal movements, determined their village sites, and designated their trading partners.

As feudalism depended on relatively large populations in small areas to work properly, it never fully developed in Acadia. The Acadians were usually able to ignore their seigneurs, just as they would ignore the English when they eventually became their new masters.

The Acadians were an agrarian people who tilled tidal marshlands, which they had reclaimed through an extensive system of dykes. In the main, they were not interested in government, but just wanted to get on with their peaceful, pastoral existence. Yet they were caught in the middle of a great power conflict in which they had no interest. They did not have much desire to obey the French governors at Port Royal, and happily traded with New Englanders, even though it was forbidden.

British interest in Acadia usually played out through New England. To many New Englanders, Acadia offered trade opportunities, rich fishing grounds, and, eventually, cultivated farmlands on which to settle the American colonies' growing population. In 1654, New England naval forces under Puritan merchant Robert Sedgwick attacked and plundered Acadian forts at Port Royal and on the Saint John and Penobscot rivers.

America was called New France. At its greatest extent, at the beginning of the eighteenth century, New France roughly corresponded to modern-day Quebec, Ontario, and the Atlantic Provinces, together with parts of the northeastern and Great Lakes areas of the United States. The Maritime Provinces, Gaspé, and eastern Maine areas were known collectively as Acadia and its French inhabitants as Acadians. France's other major North American possession was the vast territory of Louisiana, which encompassed most of the huge Mississippi River watershed, by which New France and Louisiana were connected.

Acadian dyke lands

With Acadia now under British control, Sedgwick established an inhabitants' council, presided over by Guillaume Trahan, a steelsmith and the *syndic*, or community representative, at Port Royal. This council administered the colony under the supervision of Sedgwick's son-in-law, Captain John Leverett, and a small garrison of Massachusetts soldiers. The British governor, New Englander Sir Thomas Temple, only visited Port Royal once, and was happy to leave local matters in the hands of the Acadians. In the process, the New England idea of local self-government—conducted at town meetings by property owners and the officials whom they elected—took root among the Acadians in a rudimentary form. It was a privilege the citizens of France did not yet possess, and one that the Acadians achieved long before the future English inhabitants of the colony.

The British had taken La Tour prisoner when they captured Acadia and transferred him to England, where he worked out arrangements to pay debts incurred in Boston. In return, the British recognized his right as a baronet of Nova Scotia, as his father's heir. La Tour returned to Acadia and stayed until his death in 1666. Meanwhile, the colony remained under nominal British control until it was restored to France in 1670 by the Treaty of Breda, signed in 1667.

When French authorities returned, they noted that the Acadians were reluctant to obey directions unless they first had the opportunity to discuss it fully among themselves. They attributed this to "a certain English and Parliamentary inclination which is inspired by the frequent contact and commerce they have with Boston." Yale history professor John Mack Faragher, author of *A Great and Noble Scheme*, believes "the inhabitants also must have drawn on their own tradition of governance, their experience in communal management of dykes, for example, as well as the example of consensus decision making in Mi'kmaw society, to which they were so closely bound."

With Acadia once again a French possession, the Crown took the responsibility for appointing governors, rather than relying on the seigneurial system of leadership that had been in place up to the British conquest. Héctor d'Andigné de Grandfontaine arrived as the first royal governor in 1670, but decided to govern from Penobscot Bay. In his place, he gave Alexandre Le Borgne local authority at Port Royal and dissolved the inhabitants' council. By now the colonists were used to governing themselves and soon turned against Le Borgne and his unreasonable decrees and demands. Grandfontaine dismissed him.

Meanwhile, the Acadian population was doubling itself approximately every twenty years, mainly through natural growth, but also through additional

An Acadian girl

colonists sent out from France. In 1670, there were about four hundred Acadians; by 1686, this had grown to nearly nine hundred. As their numbers grew, they spread from the Port Royal area up the Bay of Fundy to Minas Basin and Cobequid Bay, then around Chignecto Cape to Beaubassin (near modern Amherst) on the Isthmus of Chignecto.

In 1687, Louis-Alexandre Des Friches de Meneval became governor of Acadia with new marching orders. He had directions to expand the western boundary of Acadia as far as the Kennebec River in Maine, to prevent foreigners from fishing in French waters or trading with the natives, and to strengthen Port Royal. This led to renewed fighting between New Englanders and the French, both assisted by their native allies.

In 1690, New Englanders attacked Port Royal again. An expedition from Massachusetts under William Phips captured the settlement, ostensibly in retaliation for raids from New France on New England.

Obverse of a medal commemorating the Treaty of Utrecht, 1713

Phips returned to Boston with Meneval in tow, having left the administration of the colony in the hands of a council of Acadians. The British Crown issued a proclamation incorporating Acadia into Massachusetts, but the English never occupied it. Other assaults from New England followed, usually in retaliation for raids.

In 1697, the Treaty of Ryswick returned Acadia to France for the last time. In 1704, Port Royal successfully survived a naval blockade, followed by two attacks in 1707. Then, on October 13, 1710, the French outpost fell to the English for the final time, as a combined naval and military force under Colonel Francis Nicholson, assisted by Captain Samuel Vetch, overwhelmed its defenders. The last French governor at Port Royal, Daniel d'Auger de Subercase, had managed to hold out for a week.

British Representative Government

The British installed a garrison at Port Royal, and Vetch, a Scot, became the first British administrator of Nova Scotia on the departure of French officials and soldiers, leaving about fifteen hundred Acadians to the British. Vetch remained there for a year or so, to return later as governor. The British retained Port Royal as their capital, but changed its name to Annapolis Royal in honour of their monarch, Queen Anne.

Three years later, the Treaty of Utrecht, which ended the War of the Spanish Succession, formalized the English ownership of Acadia. In accordance with that agreement, France was to cede all Acadia "within its ancient limits" to the British, although Île Royale (Cape Breton Island) and Île Saint-Jean (Prince Edward Island) were expressly excluded from the treaty.

Having retained these two islands, the French then tried to restrict the territory that made up Acadia, limiting it to peninsular Nova Scotia south of the Missaguash River on the Isthmus of Chignecto. Conveniently forgotten or ignored were the true boundaries of old Acadia. Under the original French claim, Acadia included all of present-day New Brunswick and eastern Maine, as far west as the Penobscot River, as well as most of the Gaspé Peninsula. The ownership of these territories was

Annapolis Royal in the 1700s

to remain a source of conflict between the French and English for another fifty years.

Once the British had gained possession of Nova Scotia, they created a colonial backwater by promptly neglecting it. Although the colony was now British, there were few English people in it. The British population at the time consisted of a handful of administrators to run the colony at Annapolis plus a few seasonal fishermen at Canso, in addition to a tiny garrison of soldiers and a small number of merchants at each location. The vast majority of the population was made up of Acadians—different in language and religion from the English. The governing of the colony essentially consisted of administering the Acadians.

Under the French, the Acadians had shown themselves to be a people who did not want to be governed, having no interest in the policies and conflicts that inevitably were a part of government. They simply ignored official regulations and managed their own affairs, a trait they continued to display under British rule. The Acadians were given a choice. They had one year in which to take an oath of allegiance to the British sovereign or leave the colony. As most were reluctant to do either, they became a problem—and a constant worry—for the British. Successive governors complained about the "hard, and uneasy Task" they had to govern a people who would not believe or listen to reason, "unless it comes out of the mouths of their Priests."

The governors asked the Board of Trade and Plantations—the body, in England, responsible for overseeing colonial settlement and development—how to make the English presence more secure, but little was forthcoming in the form of practical assistance. In 1719, the board agreed to guarantee the constitutional rights of Englishmen in an attempt to attract settlers.

Richard Philipps, who was governor from 1717 to 1749—and was absent from the colony for all but six of those years—was given a new commission and instructions that required him to call an assembly before laws could be passed. But the Lords of the Board of Trade added a caveat: because Nova Scotia had not been previously settled by the British, they did not consider it necessary that the commission and instructions be as extensive as those issued to other British governors in America.

The board was reluctant to commit to a settlement scheme for Nova Scotia, because such a plan invariably involved New Englanders. The Lords intended to "purge Nova Scotia of the possible taint of New England republicanism and to make it conform to the character of the more admirable Virginia." The net result was that the province remained without some British institutions because there were insufficient people to run them. When he arrived at Port Royal in April 1720, Philipps established a council—the appointed body that advised the governor—consisting of eleven officers and townsmen plus himself. But it was difficult to maintain a quorum on the council because of the small and transitory English population.

Still the colonial administrators persisted. Lieutenant-Governor Lawrence Armstrong, sitting in for an absent Philipps, suggested on two separate occasions how an assembly might be convened. In 1725 he recommended moving the seat of government from Annapolis to Canso. From the tiny, transient English population there, he proposed the appointment of a general assembly "Composed of twenty four of the principall Inhabitants to make Laws for the Good Gover^mt of the Province." Six years later, in 1731, he suggested forming an assembly that included Acadian deputies, hoping this would bring them "through their own free and voluntary act to pay a greater obedience to the Government." The board remained unconvinced.

In the end, the colony was managed for several years by the governor or his representative in his capacity as military commander, a number of councillors, the occasional order from the Board of Trade, and—surprisingly—by the laws of Virginia. An article in the original instructions to the governor had ordered that until such time as a council and assembly were practicable, he was to conform to the instructions issued to the governor of Virginia, inasmuch as they were applicable to Nova Scotia. But these were inadequate alternatives to a properly constituted assembly.

To handle emergency situations and several persistent problems, the governor and council were frequently forced to issue proclamations, which effectively became legislation by default, and were seldom overturned by the board. Meanwhile, to govern the Acadians, local arrangements were made in 1720 that formalized the annual election and functions of deputies to represent them, a practice inherited by the Acadians from the time when New Englanders controlled the colony.

The authorities were quite content to let this system continue, as it provided them with someone to receive their directions and ensure that they were carried out. In effect, the deputies, which varied from four to eight per settlement, functioned as local government for the fast-growing Acadian population (less than eighteen hundred in 1713; about ten thousand in 1749)—something that the English residents did not yet enjoy. British authorities also appointed Acadians to a few minor offices.

Major General Jean-Paul Mascarene

The Acadians continued to refuse to swear an oath of allegiance to the British Crown unless it was qualified by clear recognition of their freedom of religion, neutrality during wartime, and right to emigrate. In 1730, the year after he returned to the colony, Philipps succeeded in receiving qualified oaths. To obtain them, he verbally promised the Acadians that they were exempt from bearing arms—in effect recognizing their neutrality—but neglected to tell his superiors this important detail. It was a compromise that would trouble the British for the next quarter century and have disastrous consequences for the Acadians. Authorities recalled Philipps to England in 1731, although he remained governor in name until 1749.

Lawrence Armstrong ruled as lieutenant-governor until 1739, when in a "Melancholy Fitt" he stabbed himself to death. Paul Mascarene became administrator in 1740, and remained as such until Edward Cornwallis arrived in 1749. Between the final capitulation of Acadia in 1710 and the founding of Halifax in 1749, the government of Nova Scotia was hardly more than an improvised arrangement between English masters and their Acadian subjects. But while the British were doing little in their new colony, the French were proceeding with a grandiose project in the remnants of Acadia that still belonged to them: the building of a giant fortress. Its aim was to ensure that France remained a power in North America and would be able to retain what was left of its empire there.

Île Royale

Having lost Port Royal and mainland Nova Scotia, the French decided to build the new capital for Acadia on Île Royale (Cape Breton Island) and people it with new settlers. Their plans included a fortress larger and stronger than anything yet built in North America—a French Gibraltar. The new headquarters would guard the entrance to the Gulf of Saint Lawrence and—by extension—New France; encourage trade with Quebec, New England, and the West Indies; control the lucrative cod fishery; and show the rest of the world that France was still a great power. The French started to build their great fortress on a promontory on the bleak southeast coast of Cape Breton in 1720. They named it Louisbourg in honour of Louis XIV, the Sun King and great-grandfather of the ruling king, Louis XV, and made it the capital of Île Royale.

The British would not allow the Acadians to move to Cape Breton from their settlements that ringed the head of the Bay of Fundy, seeing them as a source of labour and supplies for the Annapolis garrison, as well as protection against the Mi'kmaq. In an attempt to control any such movement, the authorities forbade them to sell their property or cattle or build boats. In the end, sixty-seven families did manage to relocate to Île Royale, but generally the British need not have worried. Most Acadians were not impressed with the fog-shrouded, rocky island and were quite content to remain on the mainland, even if it was under British rule. For their part, the French made minimal attempts to entice the Acadians to move to Cape Breton and were not overly concerned that they wanted to stay on the mainland. The French authorities saw the Acadians as a sort of a fifth column that would rise up against the British during any future war between France and England.

French Colonial Government on Île Royale

Virtually all aspects of life—and death—on Île Royale were under the control of two appointed royal officials: the governor and the *commissaire-ordonnateur*, or financial administrator, known as the *intendant* in larger colonies. The governor represented the military authority, while the *commissaire-ordonnateur* represented the civil element. Although French authorities provided individuals filling these posts with clear direction on their responsibilities, in several areas there was some degree of overlap and conflict often occurred between them. At times, personal antagonism descended to such petty matters as their seats in church, the order in which they received the sacraments, and their places in processions.

Underneath the governor and *commissaire-ordonnateur* were several lesser officials, as well as a system of courts and administrative procedures. There were two important official bodies established in the colony. The superior council (created in 1717) was supposed to function primarily as a higher law court, and to register royal edicts and ordinances, while the *bailliage* (created in 1734) was a lower law court. There was also an admiralty court to handle maritime matters. In practice, it seems as if some governors and *commissaire-ordonnateurs* used the superior council as an advisory body on certain matters. Both the superior council and the *bailliage* addressed a number of different areas of colonial life, and issued regulations and local ordinances.

Although the governor was the pre-eminent individual in the colony, the *commissaire-ordonnateur* chaired the meetings of the superior council, as the administration of justice fell under his jurisdiction. In addition to these two, there were initially four other council members—three of whom were military officers. As much of the work of the council related to the main focus of the colony—fishing and commerce—in 1720, *Commissaire-ordonnateur* Jacques-Ange Le Normant de Mézy suggested adding civilians to the council to bring the number of counsellors to fifteen. Although the ministry of the marine, the department that directed the navy and French colonial affairs, did not agree with such a massive change, by 1725 two civilians had been added.

In some cases—perhaps a majority—the decisions and directions of the superior council may have been prompted by demands from certain interests, such as fishing proprietors. Parks Canada historian A. J. B. (John) Johnston, who has studied Louisbourg for many years and written several books about it, once viewed the whole structure as a top-down, authoritarian model, but now believes it was quite responsive to local issues and situations. Although there were limits and the superior council was far from a democratic institution—no one voted on its membership or decisions—it did react to concerns raised by residents, at least some of the time.

The colonial authorities at Louisbourg were not averse to graft and corruption. Several made small fortunes by selling goods from France to New Englanders, and then buying them back at greatly inflated prices, which usually included a kickback. Officers, officials, and merchants took a hefty cut on everything sold, from liquor in the taverns to the services of the girls in the brothels.

Despite the money-making opportunities offered by a stint at Louisbourg, it was a placement universally despised by civil ser-

THE FORTRESS OF LOUISBOURG

It took several years to build Louisbourg, in the process draining the French treasury of several million livres. In fact, Louisbourg was either being built or repaired continuously throughout its lifetime, due to the ravages of weather, the poor quality work of unskilled soldiers, or the destruction caused by enemy bombardment. Intended to be impregnable, it contained eight bastions in three kilometres of three-metre-thick, ten-metre-high stone walls, which enclosed the fort's twenty-three hectares. The walls were fitted with embrasures for 148 cannons, including big 24- and 42-pounders. The rocky, surf-pounded shore stretched along three of its four sides, providing additional protection, while a string of shoals narrowed the harbour entrance to less than four hundred metres.

In that entrance were thirty guns on Battery Island, with twenty-eight 42-pounders and smaller artillery pieces on the far side of the harbour in Grand Battery. Three kilometres to the

→

→

south, at Garbarus Bay, temporary emplacements prevented the landing of troops, while swampy ground on the landward side of the fortress prevented the approach of any enemy heavy artillery. The fort's two hundred-plus cannons and twenty mortars were supplemented by the guns of French ships in port. In time, the population of Louisbourg grew to around 6,200 souls, many of them bored, drunk, or both.

The New England expedition against Cape Breton, 1745

vants. Whenever possible they returned to France on the flimsiest of excuses. Several governors were absent for up to two years during their appointments. The ordinary soldiers, who could not escape the interminable boredom of Louisbourg, generally turned to drink, on which they spent their salaries and money from part-time jobs, some even selling pieces of their equipment on the black market to get a few francs to buy alcohol.

New Englanders regarded Louisbourg as a threat to their security and chaffed impatiently to do something about it. A successful French raid on Canso, which resulted in the surrender of its small British garrison, the capture of military and civilian prisoners, and the burning of fishermen's shacks and cod-drying racks, coupled with an unsuccessful attack on Annapolis, provided the New Englanders with an excuse for action. Led by Massachusetts Governor William Shirley and wealthy lumberman William Pepperell—who was made a brigadier for the occasion—an expeditionary force of 4,270 volunteer militiamen was recruited and assembled to capture Louisbourg. No one was more surprised than the New Englanders when the

The capture of Louisbourg, 1745

fortress surrendered after a seven-week siege on June 15.

The New Englanders' rejoicing was muted when they learned that they had to remain to garrison the fortress over the winter. Additionally, they had to repair the damage their bombardment had caused, in anticipation of a French attack to recapture their lost fortress in the spring. The men from Massachusetts soon suffered under the same appalling conditions that had distressed the French: poor quality and insufficient food that caused scurvy and dysentery; cramped, stone-cold barracks; and bedding that swarmed with lice. About nine hundred were felled by sickness, nearly seven times as many as died in the attack. Very shortly, the New Englanders would come to detest not only Louisbourg, but their British masters for what they did with it.

French victories in Europe in 1747 led to peace the next year and the signing of the Treaty of Aix-la-Chapelle. Louisbourg—now repaired by New Englanders and the British—was returned to France in exchange for the removal of French forces from the Netherlands and French recognition of the Protestant House of Hanover as the legitimate rulers of Britain, which demolished the last claims of the Catholic Stuarts to the British throne. To cinch such a good deal, the French quickly threw in their trading post at Madras in India. Needless to say, the New Englanders were thoroughly disgusted with their mother country's unilateral decision, widely seen as a double-cross. These feelings would be reinforced over the next few years, culminating in the American Revolution.

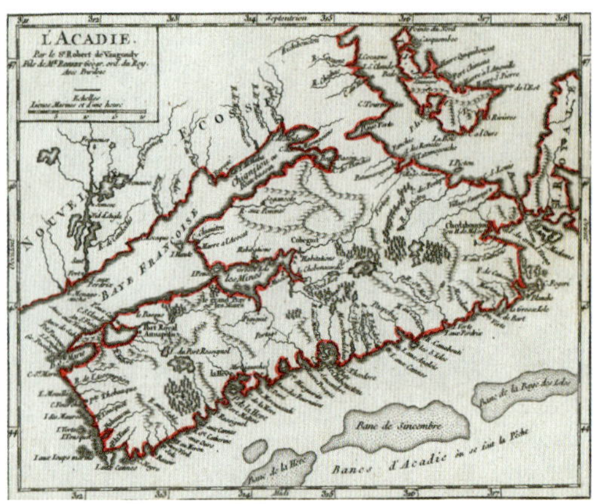

Map of L'Acadie, originally published in 1748–49

The return of Louisbourg to the French had a profound effect upon the future of Nova Scotia. Never happy with their situation at Annapolis Royal, English governors there had long been agitating for a major British presence on the Atlantic coast of the colony to offset Louisbourg. They were strongly supported in this desire by vocal New Englanders who viewed the renewed French presence with alarm and wanted a British fort to guard their eastern flank. With the massive fortress now back in French hands—and in response to this continuing agitation—the British decided to move their capital. In the spring of 1749, His Majesty's Government voted monies and commanded a plan for a settlement at *Kjipuktuk*—the great long harbour of the Mi'kmaq. The founding of the new settlement suddenly gave the question of how Nova Scotia was to be governed a new impetus and importance.

CHAPTER 3
THE FIGHT FOR REPRESENTATIVE GOVERNMENT

The Founding of Halifax

THE PATH TO REPRESENTATIVE GOVERNMENT in Nova Scotia was widened considerably with the founding of Halifax. In the summer of 1749, Colonel Edward Cornwallis and 2,576 settlers, soldiers, and staff arrived in thirteen vessels at the great long harbour, the first large-scale attempt at English settlement in the colony. The expedition resulted in the founding of Halifax and the permanent settlement of Chebucto (the English rendering of *Kjipuktuk*).

The tiny colony was named in honour of Lord Halifax, president of the Board of Trade and Plantations, the organization that directed and oversaw the town's establishment. The creation of this instant community by the conscious act of a government—rather than by chance, haphazardly—was unique, and the first major step in the English settlement of Nova Scotia and the establishment of its own government.

Halifax's first settlers were largely private citizens who had come to Nova Scotia to obtain a grant of land on which to establish themselves and their families. Although a few merchants accompanied them, many businessmen quickly showed up from New England, intent on making

Susannah Salter, wife of Malachy Salter, an early Halifax settler

The man who founded Halifax was a career soldier with influential family connections. When he arrived in Nova Scotia as its governor, thirty-seven-year-old Colonel the Honourable Edward Cornwallis was an eighteen-year veteran of the army, a Member of Parliament, and the twin brother of the Archbishop of Canterbury. He had fought against the French in 1745 and participated in the near slaughter of Highland Scots at Culloden a few months later. Contemporaries described Cornwallis as "a brave sensible young man of great temper and good nature," as well as one of "approved courage and fidelity."

Cornwallis had the ultimate say in the choice of a location for the new settlement, and time has approved the wisdom

a fast dollar from the colonial government. Among them were men such as Malachy Salter, a young Yankee merchant who could drive a hard bargain. He set up shop on "the Beach"—as Water Street was known—where the waterfront was initially divided into land and water lots and granted to the first settlers.

Many of the settlers that arrived with Cornwallis were clearly unsuited to the daunting task of hewing their homes out of virgin wilderness. The advertisements for colonists had gone out too late in the season to attract the sturdy, reliable folk required, and in many cases it was the proverbial dregs of society that came instead, looking for a free lunch ticket. Unable or unwilling to fend for themselves, by the next summer many of those who had survived the first winter headed for the milder climes and established town sites of New England.

Cornwallis and the Executive Council

Halifax's first settlers had been promised a civil government before they left England, as well as "all the liberties, privileges and immunities enjoyed by His Majesty's subjects in any other of the Colonies and Plantations in America under His Majesty's Government." To accomplish this, Cornwallis had been directed to summon an assembly of representatives of the people as soon as he deemed it practical to do so.

As the primary steps in forming a governing body for the colony, Cornwallis appointed an executive council and moved the seat of government from Annapolis Royal to Halifax. On July 12, Paul Mascarene, who had been the administrator at Annapolis during the long absence of Governor Philipps, arrived in Halifax with his staff, having been summoned by Cornwallis. Two days later, Cornwallis organized the promised civil government by swearing in six military and civilian councillors, even though his instructions called for twelve. Their first meeting was held in the great cabin of the *Beaufort*, one of the larger transports that had carried settlers across the Atlantic. The formation of the council was announced by a general salute from the ships in harbour and "the day

The settlement of Halifax in 1750

of his choice of a hillside on the western shore of the harbour. The governor was unstinting and outspoken in his attempts to obtain additional funding for the colony from the British authorities. He brought with him a commission and set of instructions from the king that were far more comprehensive than anything issued earlier to Governor Richard Philipps, and which were the real basis of the provincial constitution.

Cornwallis left Halifax in 1752, in ill health and disillusioned by difficulties with the Board of Trade. He recommended his army career, and was promoted major general in 1757 and lieutenant general in 1760. In 1762, he was appointed governor at Gibraltar, where he remained until his death in 1776. The American Revolution had broken out the previous year, a long, drawn out campaign that eventually saw his more famous nephew— Lieutenant General Charles Cornwallis—surrender his army in 1781 to combined American and French forces at Yorktown, the last major battle of the war.

was devoted to festivity and amusement." The oak table around which the councillors sat is still used in Province House—today the seat of Nova Scotia's government.

Although the disparate group that formed the council probably reflected a wide cross-section of Nova Scotia inhabitants at the time—and could be considered as fairly representative—it did not meet the direction of the Lords of the Board of Trade and Plantations for an elected assembly. Such an assembly was to be chosen by freeholders in each township, who at the time were overwhelmingly concentrated at Halifax. Cornwallis considered this was too limited a group for writs to be issued and no election was called. As a result, the governor and council continued to act as a temporary legislative authority.

Cornwallis's actions upset many of the settlers and 250 of them signed a formal grievance over the delay. When the protestors were told this action might jeopardize the province's parliamentary grants, they dropped it for the moment, to wait for "a fitter opportunity." It never came during Cornwallis's time as governor.

Cornwallis also ended the long-established practice of appointing Acadian deputies, announcing that he was putting an end to the pretence that the Acadians had the privilege of petition or the right to representation.

Because military officials were being assigned to each district, the governor decided the deputy system had outlived its usefulness and that it was time to terminate "such a useless custom." From now on, Acadians were to deal with the government only through the British senior officer in their district. He also banned public meetings, as he was aware of "the bad consequences of those frequent assemblies, where often the most honest people are led astray by some seditious persons." The always uneasy relationship between the Acadians and their British masters deteriorated considerably, but far, far worse was to come.

Peregrine Hopson succeeded Cornwallis in 1752. His instructions stated he was to call an assembly when the townships (i.e., more than one) had fifty or more families settled in each of them. Meanwhile, new settlers were desperately needed to replace those who had died or fled during the first winter. The first "Foreign Protestants"—German, French, and Swiss subjects of King George III from European principalities connected with the Crown that were suffering severe economic problems, religious persecution, or war—had arrived in 1750. Many settled in Halifax's northern suburbs, while others later moved on to found Lunenburg in 1753, under the control of Charles Lawrence. As most of Lunenburg's settlers were foreigners—who

Benjamin Green was another Massachusetts native, as well as a Harvard graduate. He came to Nova Scotia with the New England force that captured Louisbourg in 1745 and remained there as a government official. He held several important public offices in Halifax.

Hugh Davidson was an Englishman who arrived with Cornwallis and became the first provincial secretary. He returned to England the next year under charges of trading in settlers' supplies.

John Salusbury was another Englishman who sailed with Cornwallis, but as a protégé of Lord Halifax who could not be ignored—despite his dissipation and argumentative nature. He seems to have taken little part in the affairs of the colony and returned to England in 1753.

Governor Peregrine Thomas Hopson replaced Edward Cornwallis

A view of Lunenburg from Battery Point

needed seven years' residence in the province to qualify as electors—it did not meet the requirement to be considered a township.

Meanwhile, an expansion to the eastern side of Halifax Harbour also occurred that summer, when 353 settlers arrived on the *Alderney* to establish the new community of Dartmouth. The most desirable lots—those on the waterfront—were taken first. They were safer, made contact with Halifax easier, and were closest to the fishery.

Charles Lawrence and the Struggle for Representative Government

Hopson left Halifax in late 1753 after only fourteen months in office, without an assembly having been called. One of his few accomplishments was to succeed in getting a chief justice appointed for the colony: New England–born, British-trained Jonathan Belcher. By the time Hopson departed, he and his successor, Charles Lawrence, seemed to regard the order directing an assembly as more along the lines of some sort of acceptance or recognition of the possibility of doing so, should it ever be necessary. Meanwhile, other pressures were mounting for the election of an assembly; one legal and one popular.

The first pressure for an assembly came from the Board of Trade and

Plantations. Its members questioned the legal propriety of legislation enacted solely by the governor and council. Their instructions to the governor—and his commission—assumed that the only way to make laws were with the assent of an elected assembly. The concerns of the Lords—"some difficulties in relation to our Laws"—were conveyed to Lawrence in October 1754 with the arrival of Belcher as chief justice of the colony. Lawrence immediately advised the board that he and the council considered this a matter of the utmost importance and they would study it most carefully.

The "Conquered Colony" Decision

Chief Justice Belcher spent the rest of that fall contemplating the need for an assembly. In the end, his opinion was a masterly proposal—for maintaining the status quo. He decided that the laws promulgated by the governor and council were fully warranted and that an assembly was not a legal necessity. He based this finding on the fact that Nova Scotia was a conquered colony—an old idea based on the distinction between settled and conquered colonies.

According to this view, colonists who came out and settled a colony carried with them the laws of England—as far as they applied to local conditions—and continued to be entitled to all their legal rights and safeguards

→

without his direction, influence, actions, and administrative talent.

Lawrence commanded a brigade in the second successful expedition against Louisbourg in 1758. During his last years as governor, he concentrated on settling new immigrants, mostly from New England, and building a larger governor's house on the site of the one-storey cabin erected for Cornwallis. When he died in office in 1760, he was honoured with a monument in Halifax's Saint Paul's Church. Most historians agree that Lawrence enjoyed a successful career in the army and government. Almost uniquely for his time, it was without the support of an influential patron. No known portrait of Lawrence exists.

as subjects of the Crown. They still owed allegiance to the sovereign, under whose protection they fell. They were only subject to laws and taxes approved by a legislature in which they were represented—or by the sovereign in Parliament.

Belcher noted the same principle did not apply to the people of a colony that was acquired by conquest or by another country surrendering it. Its citizens were without rights and the royal prerogative was essentially unlimited. The Crown could make whatever laws it wanted, without the people's consent, for their regulation and government through orders-in-council. Belcher went on to state that the sovereign could delegate this power to others, as was the case in the commission to the governor of Nova Scotia, who governed in conjunction with the council.

But Belcher didn't stop at this. Although he agreed that the governor's commission and instructions indicated that laws could only be enacted with the assent of an assembly, he noted that they also stated that there could be no assembly until the province was "entirely Planted and Settled." Yet, he argued, laws were necessary until that state was achieved. He also pointed out the instructions to the governor were vague: no specific time had been given by which election writs were to be issued, and writs were only to be issued once any towns had fifty families living there.

Belcher argued from this latter restriction, which specified "towns," that at least two townships of fifty families had to be established before an election could be called. At the time, Halifax alone met this requirement—the people in other settlements did not meet voter qualifications of religion or citizenship. Roman Catholic Acadians lived at Minas and Pisiquid (Windsor), while Germans and other foreigners made up Lunenburg. Given the colony's need for laws despite only having one township—and with the establishment of any other townships impractical at the time and up to the governor's authority in any case—Belcher concluded that the governor and council had the full authority to pass laws until an assembly became necessary.

His Excellency Jonathan Belcher, chief justice of Nova Scotia

Governor Lawrence agreed with Chief Justice Belcher, while claiming not to be an expert in matters of legislative authority. As well, he pointed out to the Board of Trade that the power of the governor and council had not been questioned previously in the province. Finally, he expressed concerns that if an assembly were to be called now, it would be dominated by the New England merchants at Halifax, a group he believed had profit rather than patriotism as their primary motivation.

Legal Opinion of the Board of Trade

On March 31, 1755, the Board of Trade referred the matter of Belcher's views on a Nova Scotia assembly to the British attorney general and

A view of Fort Cumberland, 1755

solicitor general for a legal opinion. A month later, the Crown's law officers stated "that the Governor and Council alone are not authorized by His Majesty to make Laws till there can be an Assembly." The board promptly forwarded a copy of this decision to Lawrence (it did not reach Halifax until July), with direction to prepare a plan to summon an assembly in concert with Belcher and report the details as soon as possible.

Although the board noted that it might be difficult and inconvenient to form a legislature given the existing state of the colony, once British legal authorities ruled that the governor and council did not have the power to enact any laws, their Lords could not see how the government of the province could continue without an elected assembly. Since the validity of the laws passed by the governor and council appeared not to have been questioned to date, their Lords also asked that the legal opinion should not be made public for the continued peace and welfare of the colony until an assembly could be convened and it passed an indemnification for all acts done under the previous laws, which had been enacted without proper authority.

When the board's despatch reached Halifax, the provincial authorities were engaged with a more pressing matter, one that changed the face of Nova Scotia and the ramifications of which are still felt today.

The Acadians' Fortunes Change

Until the founding of Halifax, the main task of the colonial authorities at Annapolis Royal was the supervision of the Acadians, who made up almost the entire population of Nova Scotia. With a high birth rate, their numbers had grown from a few hundred original settlers to about ten thousand by 1749. The indifference the Acadians displayed towards authorities when the colony was French only worsened once their new British masters took over. They disregarded official regulations and continued to manage their own affairs, much to the frustration of English governors and administrators.

After Britain returned Louisbourg to France in 1748, both sides set out to strengthen their positions in Acadia. To solidify their claim to the disputed parts of the colony north of the Missaguash River, the French fortified the mouth of the Saint John River in 1749 and built Fort Beauséjour and Fort

Reading the expulsion order to the Acadians in the parish church at Grand Pré in 1755

Gaspéreau on the Isthmus of Chignecto in 1751. Then they pressured the Acadians living on the isthmus to move north of the river, into present-day New Brunswick. Some Acadians, sensing that their fortunes were about to change, emigrated to Île Saint-Jean (Prince Edward Island) instead.

French–English relations enjoyed a period of qualified peace in Nova Scotia at the time, but the same could not be said for the rest of the continent. The French and English—both using other European mercenaries, native allies, and colonists—were sparring on the fringes of their territories along the Great Lakes, the Ohio River Valley, and upper New York State. The conflict spilled over into Acadia in the summer of 1755, when a fleet sailed from Boston carrying a force of two thousand New England militiamen under the command of Colonel Robert Monckton, a British regular, and Lieutenant Colonel John Winslow. Their destination was the Isthmus of Chignecto at the head

Lieutenant-Colonel John Winslow, who helped expel the Acadians

of the Bay of Fundy, where the French occupied Fort Beauséjour on what they maintained was the border between their territory and Nova Scotia.

Capturing Fort Saint John along the way, the expedition landed below Beauséjour on June 2 and immediately besieged it. Inside the star-shaped fort, Louis de Verger commanded 150 regulars and about 300 Acadians he had coerced into joining him—far less than the 1,000 Monckton expected. The British bombardment began on June 13, the Acadians threatened mutiny, and on June 16 Verger surrendered. Monckton immediately marched across the narrow peninsula to its Northumberland Strait side, where he accepted the surrender of Fort Gaspéreau without a struggle. The British now completely controlled the border.

Emboldened by these victories and at the urging of the council (which contained three New England merchants) and Governor William Shirley of Massachusetts (who coveted the Acadians' rich farmlands for his overcrowded people), Governor Lawrence decided to present the Acadians with an ultimatum: they could no longer exist as so-called "French Neutrals," but would have to swear allegiance to the British Crown—which included taking up arms for the sovereign—or leave their farms forever. It was a threat the Acadians had heard several times before, but they had always managed to reach an accommodation with the British without actually taking the oath.

Cornwallis had attempted to get the Acadians to take an unqualified oath of allegiance, but relented when they threatened to leave Nova Scotia. His successor, Hopson, chose to let sleeping dogs lie and did not pursue the issue. Naturally enough, the Acadians assumed their claims of neutrality would continue to be respected. But Lawrence fully intended on carrying through with his threat, although its legality was highly questionable at best and unlawful at worst. Unfortunately, the Board of Trade had implicitly acquiesced to this decision when, in August 1754, Lawrence advised them that if the Acadians refused to take the oath, it would be better to remove them from Nova Scotia and replace them with British colonists.

The expulsion of the Acadians from Grand Pré

Although Cornwallis had dismissed the Acadian deputies during his time as governor, in the summer of 1755 the Acadians were directed to again nominate representatives. Though they didn't know it at the time, it was for one final and tragic act. The chosen deputies were summoned before Lawrence and the council at Halifax, where they rejected their last opportunity to take an unconditional oath. This final democratic action on the part of the Acadians sealed their fate.

News of a British defeat in the Ohio Valley steeled Lawrence's resolve and with the council's concurrence he decided to disperse the Acadians. The draconian deportation began immediately under the supervision of Monckton, Winslow, and Major John Handfield. The largely peaceful farmers were forcibly deported and scattered throughout Britain's other New World colonies (mostly along the Atlantic seaboard or Louisiana) and to France. They were allowed to take their clothing, money, and some personal belongings, but their homes, livestock, and farms were forfeited to the Crown and often destroyed by British troops.

Le Grand Dérangement—the Expulsion of the Acadians—was one of the first examples of ethnic cleansing in the modern colonial period, which began around 1500. Starting in October 1755 and continuing until 1763, about three-quarters of the entire Acadian population—French in language and Roman Catholic in religion—were expelled from the colony. Families were split up as the British herded them onto ships, many never to be reunited again. Some managed to escape by fleeing to the wilderness of present-day New Brunswick and Prince Edward Island, or to Quebec. In later years many of them returned, attracted by a change in government policy, which encouraged their repatriation.

Two and a half centuries after the event, the British implicitly recognized the error of Lawrence's decision. In 2003, Queen Elizabeth II issued a Royal Proclamation that "acknowledged" British responsibility for the deportation and regretted its "tragic consequences," although it did not apologize for it.

Chapter 4
The First Legislative Assembly

The Chief Justice's Plan

GOVERNOR CHARLES LAWRENCE AND CHIEF Justice Jonathan Belcher did not discuss the British law officers' ruling on the need for an assembly until October, undoubtedly distracted by the Acadian problem. Belcher quickly drew up a proposal calling for an assembly and both men sent copies of it to England, the governor's on December 8, 1755, and the chief justice's on December 24. Belcher conformed to the legal finding. He recommended calling an assembly as soon as possible, especially to overcome any objections to the present way of governing the colony by those who came out as settlers on the promise of the same privileges as enjoyed in the other colonies. He also felt an assembly would smooth the progress of settling the lands so recently vacated by the Acadians, and recommended that the assembly be convened before granting land at Minas, Pisiquid, and Chignecto.

Belcher did not believe it was practical yet to constitute an assembly in the customary manner with people from the townships. He proposed the first assembly be made up of twelve members from the province at large. Once townships were established, the colony could be divided into counties (it was one large county at the time), which would be represented in the assembly. When towns were large enough, they too could elect members.

Belcher recommended as qualification to vote a personal estate of thirty pounds or a freehold (owned) property worth two pounds a year and suggested the assembly last for three years, to prevent the confusion annual elections might cause to the government. At the time—as was the practice elsewhere—both the electors and the elected could only be men. Belcher also thought that non-residents should be eligible to run for the assembly, in this way ensuring "the principal and best approved Gentlemen would be return'd as Representatives."

The Battle Begins

While the legal opinion and the Board of Trade's direction on the necessity of an assembly had convinced Belcher, Lawrence did not share his chief justice's view. As far as he was concerned, the province was simply not ready for an assembly, as Halifax was the only place large enough to be entitled to representatives. He felt that an assembly would hinder the effective administration of Nova Scotia.

Lawrence did not mince his words. In a letter to Lord Halifax, he showed his true colours, which seemed to indicate some disdain for the general population: "I know nothing so likely to obstruct and disconcert all measures for the publick Good," he wrote, "as the foolish squabbles that are attendant upon Elections and the impertinent opinions that will be propagated afterwards amongst the multitude by Persons qualified in their own imaginations only as able Politicians."

Although Lawrence accepted the legal necessity of an assembly because of the invalidity of the colony's present laws, paradoxically he saw no requirement for an immediate change. He maintained that all laws approved by the governor and council had been necessary for the regulation of Halifax and the encouragement of business. In any case, most of them had been made at the request of merchants or the people concerned and none of them had ever been questioned, as far as he knew. Lawrence also pointed out that a similar situation had prevailed in the early days of Virginia, when the governor and council passed laws of their own accord.

Lawrence wrote that Belcher's plan was based on a promise made to the original settlers of Halifax that they would have an assembly. Although governors since Cornwallis had been instructed to convene such a legislature with two elected members from each township, as Halifax was the only town qualified to elect representatives, there were not enough to form an assembly. He then argued that the promise had not "been broke through," merely that "its performance not yet become possible, by the Circumstances of the Province."

Lawrence also objected to Belcher's proposal for electing twelve members at large from across Nova Scotia, feeling it might set a precedent. He felt most of them would be Halifax businessmen, who were more interested in mercantile matters, rather than the landowners outside the town, on whom the security of the colony depended. The governor stated that if their Lordships considered it necessary to convene an assembly, he needed their full instructions, which he would follow immediately. He then raised the matter of expenses, wondering if the province could afford an assembly, which required a building in which to meet, as well as a clerk and other officials. "People here, in general," he added, "are not in a condition of Contributing any sum of money, to defray such an expense."

Lawrence and Belcher's correspondences were the beginning of a transatlantic debate that lasted almost three years, which was carried out through letters to and from the Board of Trade. By the end of that period, many citizens in Halifax had become aware of what had transpired, and they began a campaign of complaint, accusation, and agitation against the governor and council. Those who opposed Lawrence were not averse to stretching the truth to the point of blatant lies, and corresponded directly with the Board of Trade to voice their concerns.

Meanwhile, on March 25, 1756, the Lords responded to the letter in which Lawrence had critiqued Belcher's plan for an assembly. They refuted all of the governor's arguments point by point, while leaving certain matters to his discretion. But their minds were made up on the necessity for an assembly and they awaited the governor's notification that he had convened it. Unbelievably, Lawrence refused to summon an assembly immediately.

Lawrence offered several reasons for not issuing election writs. These included the unsuitableness of the idea, the general satisfaction of most people with the present system, the lack of precise instructions from His Majesty, his own preoccupation with the war with France, guerrilla warfare with the Mi'kmaq and the remaining Acadians, and the prevention of the return of deported Acadians. While all of this was true, most of Lawrence's points were not enough to prevent the calling of an assembly. When word filtered down to the populace that he was refusing to follow instructions, most people were upset by his arrogant and arbitrary action. Some of them took action on their own.

Even before the Lords of the Board of Trade received Lawrence's reply to their letter of March 25, they received a petition from Nova Scotians complaining about the lack of an assembly and the inconvenience it caused. The Lords followed this up with another letter to Lawrence, expressing the hope that he had put their earlier direction into action. While they believed that Nova Scotians enjoyed their rights and liberties to the full under the government in effect in the province, until an assembly was established they felt that "malevolent and ill designing Men will take the occasion to complain and misrepresent things to the prejudice of the Colony, and even the best disposed of His Majesty's Subjects there will be uneasy under the present form of Government."

Lawrence's Intransigence

The governor received this letter on July 8, 1756, before he had replied to the Lords' missive from March. Proceeding at a glacial pace, Lawrence took from August to October to draft a reply to the Board of

Trade. He included a comparative analysis of Belcher's proposals and the board's response, along with detailed remarks as to why he had not followed their direction. If nothing else, Charles Lawrence was gutsy—and not prepared to be rushed into anything with which he did not agree.

Lawrence went back to Governor Cornwallis's time to explain why an assembly had not been called. As he saw it, it would have been both inexpedient and impractical for Cornwallis to have immediately established an assembly when he founded Halifax. It was equally inexpedient for his successors to have done so, because there was not sufficient change in circumstances from the early days of the town to warrant it. He pointed out that many of the most influential men who had signed a petition for an assembly during Cornwallis's tenure now believed it would have been the wrong thing to do back then. Lawrence did not believe that any well-disposed persons had signed the petition the Lords had received, unless because of the pretences of the "malevolent and ill designing Men" their Lordships had mentioned, but in any case he did not think they still felt that way.

Lawrence also referred to the perilous state of affairs with the Mi'kmaq—soldiers had been scalped at Chignecto—which indicated a need for an adequate garrison on the isthmus. Similarly, farmers in the Lunenburg area were in terror after the scalping of the Payzant family on an island in Mahone Bay. At a time when troops were most needed to secure against such depredations, two thousand New England soldiers were being recalled from Nova Scotia. The dangers and the lack of soldiers prevented New Englanders from settling in the colony.

Lawrence further objected to Belcher's proposal to deprive the non-British Lunenburg settlers of the opportunity to sit in the first assembly. He also contrasted the instructions of His Majesty to earlier governors with those the board had issued to him. While the king's instructions clearly stated that assembly members could only be elected for townships by their freeholders—an impracticability given the province's present circumstances—the board's direction was that members of the first assembly could be elected from the entire province as one county, which accorded with Belcher's idea. As this latter direction was contrary to His Majesty's instructions, before he could act upon them, he would need additional instructions from the king.

For good measure, Lawrence included a litany of other excuses, including the fact that Lord Loudoun, the commander-in-chief for America, had ordered the colonial governors to confer with him in New York, and that Chief Justice Belcher had been away on a lengthy absence in New England on private business and had needed to devote himself to Supreme Court duties on his return. Lawrence then promised the Lords that he would consult with Belcher on the most expedient way of putting the proposal into effect with the least inconvenience, knowing how strongly the Lords had urged the whole matter. But Lawrence had not yet thrown in all his chips.

Lawrence's Plan

On December 3, 1756, Lawrence placed the whole matter of an assembly before his council. They discussed it over the course of a few meetings and devised a new plan for representative government. On January 3, 1757, the council passed the necessary resolutions to make the assembly a reality. The new plan called for a House of Assembly of twenty-two members. Twelve would be elected to represent the province at large until it was divided into counties, four to represent Halifax township, two to represent Lunenburg township, and one each to represent Dartmouth, Lawrencetown, Annapolis Royal, and Cumberland townships. Once other townships had twenty-five qualified electors, they would also be entitled to a representative. Only the governor's order was now necessary to issue the writ. But instead, Lawrence went to Boston to discuss the year's upcoming campaigns against the French with Lord Loudoun.

On his return, Lawrence claimed he was too busy with Loudoun's long-delayed preparations for an assault against Louisbourg to do anything about an assembly. Then, in August, he abruptly turned over the administration to Chief Justice Belcher, while he went to Chignecto on Loudoun's orders to relieve the troops there and put the defences in order.

When Lawrence returned from the Chignecto frontier, he found a letter from the Board of Trade waiting for him in which their Lordships expressed confidence in his justice and integrity. They also agreed that it would be futile to attempt to encourage New Englanders to settle in Nova Scotia while the colony was "so vexed and harassed" by the French and Mi'kmaq and had no desire to press him in this matter further than the province's circumstances would permit. But they added that the same reasons for not bringing in New England settlers did altogether "operate against calling an Assembly, concerning which we have given our Opinion so fully." They went on to explain that their direction for an assembly had nothing to do with any claims of grievances or the denial of any rights and liberties. Rather, it had been their view long before the petition arrived from Halifax.

Lawrence did not reply to the Lords until November 9, 1757. In his letter he expressed satisfaction with the board's letter but clearly stated he would continue his opposition to an assembly until "some happy change in the face of American affairs promises more success in an undertaking of so much moment." He noted that his inquiries in Boston into reports that the reason for a lack of New England settlers taking up the lands vacated by the Acadians was due to the lack of an assembly had shown this was not the case. He stated that the people he had recently asked for advice considered calling an assembly in the present "state of hostilities with so dangerous and near a neighbour" to be wildly unrealistic. Lawrence closed his letter by declaring that if their Lordships still wanted an assembly in these circumstances, he would carry out the plan he and the council had devised the previous winter, without a moment's delay.

Petitions, Pleas, and Pamphlets

By now, Lawrence's obstinacy and procrastination over the matter of an assembly had become known to Nova Scotians, and many responded with a barrage of abuse against the governor. Some of it was justified; some was pure fabrication. Complaints about the assembly spilled over into other areas of Lawrence's responsibilities, leading to charges of mismanagement and favouritism at the hospital. People took action. In 1756, there was an address to Lord Halifax, president of the Board of Trade, a presentment (formal statement made under oath) by the grand jury at Halifax, and two printed pamphlets complaining about Lawrence's leadership.

The next year the complaints mushroomed, and included an address to the governor calling for the electoral writ to be issued; a petition and letter to the lieutenant-governor; a letter from Belcher and three other council members to the Board of Trade complaining about the delay in calling an assembly and of ill-treatment at the hands of the governor; the election of a committee of Halifax free-holders; the appointment of an agent in London for the freeholders and a letter from them to him, as well as to Lord Halifax; a memorial (statement of facts accompanying a petition) from the grand jury to the Board of Trade; an anonymous letter to the board; and charges against Lawrence of illegal and arbitrary actions made by five Halifax citizens. Although many of the accusations were unfounded, there was a common thread that ran through all of them: the governor's arrogance, arbitrariness, and stubborn opposition to an assembly.

The two 1756 pamphlets tell a tale of Lawrence and his council—most of whom were military men when they should have been civilians—exercising complete control. The writers complained that a lack of representative government, fear of French attacks, and the military members on the council were obstacles to settlement in Nova Scotia. The presence of army officers resulted in parliamentary grants going toward military uses instead of the general improvement of the province, while members of the military filled civil posts. Troops were allowed to run rampant. They had no wood allowance for fires, and so they stole firewood, fences, and even lumber from houses.

The writers proposed a simple remedy for these evils: removing all military officers from civil appointments and replacing them with interested citizens, as well as fully establishing civil government, with all its branches, giving Nova Scotians rights and privileges equal to those of other colonists.

The 1757 documents presented a similar picture. During Lawrence's absence in Boston, the petition addressed to the lieutenant-governor asked for the immediate issuance of a writ. Although it received widespread support and was signed by 204 people, the lieutenant-governor was unwilling to act on his own initiative.

At meetings in January and February 1758, the Board of Trade decided the issue. The freeholders' London agent, John Paris, presented their case, expanding on the points made in their letter to Lord Halifax. Key among these were the council clique's control of all matters, the flaws of Lawrence's plan for an assembly, and his delay in calling it. Some thirteen months had elapsed since the plan was drawn up, an inordinate amount of time. The governor's plan for representation from the five locations outside of Halifax also drew criticism. Cumberland and Annapolis were under the control of military men, Lawrencetown had three settlers, and Lunenburg's residents were still two years away from being entitled to vote.

The Board of Trade held several meetings at which they questioned Paris and other witnesses. The Lords saw the citizens' petition as having two parts: one stressing the need for an assembly, the other consisting of complaints against Lawrence and his cronies. On February 3, they announced their decision: they would direct Lawrence to call an assembly immediately. They also asked Paris to list the charges against each officer on the council, with supporting evidence. As he lacked the personal knowledge to do this, the board decided they could not address this issue at the time.

An Assembly—Finally

The board drafted a letter to Lawrence on February 7, 1758, clearly stating its intentions regarding an assembly: "it should be immediately carried into execution." Total membership was to be twenty-two representatives, from townships with more than fifty settled families (only Halifax and Lunenburg met this requirement at the time) and as many at large from across the rest of the province to bring the numbers up to twenty-two. Once any other townships reached fifty families, they would be entitled to send two representatives and the numbers at large would be reduced proportionally.

The letter arrived in Halifax on May 8 and Lawrence replied that he would carry out the board's orders as soon as he could. Although he was part of the operation to capture Louisbourg—where he was to command a brigade—Lawrence summoned the council on May 20 to amend the plan they had drawn up in January 1757. Halifax would have four members, Lunenburg two, and the province at large sixteen. The return of the writs (documents authorizing polling officers to conduct elections, declare results, and report them) was not due until October 2, double the usual sixty days, because of the Louisbourg expedition. Church of England Reverend Jean-Baptiste Moreau in Lunenburg was told to inform his parishioners that taking the sacrament was a prerequisite for qualification as an elector, while Sebastian Zouberbuhler was dispatched there to hold a naturalization court.

Nova Scotia's first election was held in the summer of 1758. Only one poll book has survived, from Lunenburg, dated July 31. In its pages are recorded the elections of Alexander Kedie and Philip Knaut over five other candidates.

On October 2, nineteen of the twenty-two elected representatives met in the modest courthouse at the corner of Argyle and Buckingham

The Nova Scotia assembly met for the first time in the courthouse in Halifax on October 2, 1758

streets in Halifax to convene the first elected legislative assembly in what eventually became Canada. More than half the members were from New England, and some of them had been among those who had petitioned for an assembly. Of the three members not present, only one later took his seat, so the seats of the other two were declared vacant. On January 10, 1759, Lawrence issued a writ commanding the first by-election in Canada to fill them.

For the first time in the post-contact history of the province, the people of Nova Scotia had chosen others to represent them on a formal, recognized basis, one which would be repeated at regular intervals and which continues today. Through these representatives, the citizens of

A tablet erected in Province House in 1908 by the Nova Scotia government commemorating the establishment of representative government in 1758 listing the members of the first assembly

the colony—or at least those who were qualified to vote—finally had some direct input into the way they were to be governed.

This landmark had not been achieved quickly or easily. The colony had been occupied by the British since 1710, and formally became a British possession three years later. For almost half a century, the col-

The Governor's House (centre), erected by Governor Charles Lawrence on Hollis St beside the smaller original residence built for Governor Cornwallis

ony's original Mi'kmaq inhabitants and its French and English settlers had been ruled by an appointed governor and executive council, men whom the inhabitants had no voice in choosing. Even when the British government—through the Lords of the Board of Trade and Plantations—had given its direction to establish an assembly, a debate over the issue continued for another decade before the first representatives met in a formal session.

Although the creation of the assembly had occurred neither quickly nor easily, it had taken place bloodlessly. Nova Scotians did not rise in rebellion or revolution to obtain their assembly; in fact, they did not even resort to open mass protest in any form. The assembly had been achieved through the power of the written and spoken word,

Joseph Rundel, Massachusetts; merchant and brewer

Jonathan Binney, Hull, Massachusetts; merchant and shipowner (appointed to the council in 1764; later held government appointments on Saint John Island and at Canso)

Henry Ferguson; baker and trader

George Suckling; barrister and shopkeeper (later held government appointments in Quebec and the Virgin Islands)

John Burbidge, Cowes, England; farmer (arrived with Cornwallis)

Robert Campbell, England; merchant (arrived with Cornwallis)

William Pantree; merchant

Joseph Fairbanks, Sherborn, Massachusetts; merchant and trader

Philip Hammond, New England; merchant

John Fillis, Boston, Massachusetts; merchant, shipowner, and distiller

Lambert Folkers; baker and shopkeeper

Philip Knaut, Saxony; merchant and fur trader (arrived with Cornwallis; moved to Lunenburg on its founding)

→

Merchant Malachy Salter was a member of the first assembly in Nova Scotia, but did not take his seat until October 30

through civilized, rational—and sometimes seemingly endless—discussion. In many ways, this achievement marked the beginning of what was to become a very Canadian way of doing things.

Nova Scotia's House of Assembly was not the first legislative body in the British Empire; Virginia's was. Yet Nova Scotia saw the beginning of a constitutional evolution that had repercussions not only for Canada but for the entire Commonwealth. Although responsible government was further down the road—a road that would take another ninety years to travel—a major milestone in the long struggle for democracy had been achieved—and it happened in Nova Scotia.

Chapter 5
New France and New England

Early Representative Government

THE FIRST LEGISLATIVE ASSEMBLY FOR NOVA Scotia lasted from October 2, 1758, until August 13, 1759, and had two sessions. The first day of the first session was largely a pro forma affair. The assembly advised the governor they were at the courthouse and ready for business. Governor Lawrence sent two council members, Benjamin Green and Charles Morris, to swear in the assemblymen. Lawrence said he would meet the members of the assembly at his house and directed them to choose a speaker; he subsequently approved the assembly's selection of Robert Sanderson.

At the governor's house, Lawrence gave a short speech to the assembly in which he expressed his pleasure at meeting them in their new capacity, the result "of a plan some time since formed of His Majesty's Council, and by me transmitted to" Britain. He hoped they had come together to promote the "real Welfare and prosperity of the people" they represented. Lawrence then ended his speech, claiming that his military duties required his attendance elsewhere.

The assembly returned to the courthouse and hired a clerk, doorkeeper, and messenger. The members next voted unanimously to "serve without reward" for themselves. They approved a motion to prepare a bill to establish the authority of the house and set up

1760
New England Planters start to arrive

1763
Expulsion of Acadians ends; Seven Years' War ends; Cape Breton and PEI are annexed to Nova Scotia

1769
PEI becomes separate colony

1772
Yorkshire immigration begins

Representative Government in British North America

In 1758, Nova Scotia included present-day New Brunswick, but Île Saint-Jean (Prince Edward Island) and Île Royale (Cape Breton Island) remained French colonies until the fall of New France. In 1763, these French territories became British and were annexed to Nova Scotia. Prince Edward Island became a separate colony in 1769 and achieved representative government in 1773.

In 1784, due to the influx of Loyalists from the American Revolution, both New Brunswick and Cape Breton were established as separate colonies. The next year, New Brunswick elected its first assembly. Cape Breton never did get an elected assembly and in 1820 it was re-annexed to Nova Scotia.

By the Constitutional Act of 1791, part of the old French colony of Quebec was broken off and two new colonies were formed, Lower Canada and Upper Canada. The next year, both of them elected

a committee to prepare an address in reply to Lawrence's speech. The assembly then adjourned. The business of the first day of the first elected house of representatives in Canada was over.

Through their continuous efforts, the people of Nova Scotia now had a voice in running the colony, although it was far from the level of representative democracy in the province today. By law, the electors and the elected were white males aged twenty-one or older who were adherents of the established church (the Church of England) and owned property worth two pounds annually. By definition and tradition, this excluded Mi'kmaq, Acadians, blacks, and women from the process. Additionally, political parties, which could bring some discipline and cohesion to the representatives, were still unknown.

Although the establishment of the assembly barely ensured representative government, the system in Nova Scotia was even further from being responsible government. The members of the executive council were nominated by the governor or the Board of Trade and did not come from the House of Assembly. They shared the same values as the administration, usually by being appointed to official government positions or being the recipients of government patronage. They could and did sit for years, usually until they died. They were not accountable to the people or their elected representatives and did not have to resign if they lost the confidence of the assembly. In fact, there was no charter that limited the council's powers.

With the coming of the assembly, the council now performed two functions. In modern terms, these functions are roughly comparable to our federal cabinet and Senate. Today, the prime minister heads the government and is assisted by a cabinet. The cabinet consists of certain men and women appointed by the prime minister, who offer advice as well as head various government departments.

Similarly, in colonial Nova Scotia the governor headed the government and was assisted by an appointed council, many of whose members—such as the chief justice, treasurer, surveyor general, and provincial secretary—were also the heads of government departments. When presided over by the governor, the colonial council acted like a cabinet and performed the government's executive function. The only difference today is that the prime minister and the members of the cabinet must first be elected Members of Parliament (although Senators are occasionally appointed as cabinet ministers).

The second role of the council was similar to our modern Senate, whose members, like the council's, are all appointees. When the

representative assemblies. Farther west, the tiny colony of Vancouver Island elected the smallest assembly in the history of British North America in 1856, when forty voters chose seven members to represent them. British Columbia was created the next year and elected an assembly in 1863. In 1866, Vancouver Island and British Columbia were united into one colony with one legislative assembly.

As additional provinces were created after Confederation, they established their own assemblies, except for Newfoundland. When that colony became a part of Canada in 1949, it already had its own representative government, which had been created in 1832.

assembly was in session, the council was presided over by the chief justice. At these times it performed the responsibilities of an upper chamber of the legislature, like today's Senate. When it performed this function, all legislation had to be approved by the council before it became law.

As happened elsewhere, the council did not have to depend on the assembly's approval for funding; most of the government's income came from Britain and was independent of local control. Starting with Halifax's founding in 1749, the British Parliament voted most of the monies needed to run the colony through annual appropriations, a policy that continued into the 1770s. The only government income provided locally was from certain customs duties and excise taxes on spirits.

The Council of Twelve (as it came to be called derogatorily) made appointments to every salaried position in the colony except for those paid out of parliamentary grants or from customs duties, and selected almost every public official who was allowed to charge fees for the performance of his duties. In the early 1760s, annual grants from the British Parliament averaged £9,000, while local sources brought in about £2,250, largely from customs and excise duties. This gave the governor and council a large amount of independence from the elected representatives. About the only limitation on the power of the council was that it could not amend revenue and appropriation bills sent to it by the assembly; it could only approve or reject such bills in their entirety.

From the beginning the assembly and the council did not always see eye to eye, and the assembly—demonstrating its independence—was not reluctant to send bills to the council that it knew would be rejected. For example, the assembly prepared a bill that would have excluded any assemblyman or councillor from holding a paid government job. As many councillors were the salaried heads of government departments, such as chief justice, treasurer, surveyor general, and provincial secretary, the council rejected the bill. Similarly, the assembly attempted to regulate the fees of the Court of Vice-Admiralty, which ruled on shipping matters. Not only did the council reject the assembly's proposal, the court's judge refused to make his scale of fees public. The assembly declared the judge's actions in contempt of their authority and noted it could never have faith in a council in which one member was the judge of the Court of Vice-Admiralty, another was a former judge, and a third was its registrar. Council composition remained an issue that was not to be resolved until the advent of responsible government ninety years later.

In any case, for many years the assembly reflected the views of Halifax, as the majority of its members were from the capital. Their outlook was largely based on promoting measures that were good for business and commerce—including keeping an eye open for ways of making a profit from government contracts—and were often in sharp contrast to the farmers and fishermen who peopled the rest of the province. Additionally, the colony was kept under tight rein by the British government and there was little opportunity for any sentiments of liberty to flourish, as was happening in the Thirteen Colonies. The province's small and scattered population was another hindrance to the colonists meeting to discuss the government and protest its actions.

Brigadier James Wolfe wades ashore at Louisbourg, 1758

A view of Louisbourg as seen from the lighthouse when the fortress was besieged in 1758

Seven Years' War

The war between Britain and France that eventually came to be called the Seven Years' War lasted from 1756 to 1763. However, it actually began two years earlier in North America, where it was called the French and Indian War. That war began in February 1754, when the Thirteen Colonies became alarmed at an increased French presence from Quebec in the Ohio Valley. A series of battles followed to establish British control in the Ohio basin and elsewhere. One of these was the successful expedition against Fort Beauséjour.

At Louisbourg, Governor Augustin de Drucourt arrived in 1754 to take charge of the colonial administration. Drucourt, an experienced naval administrator, knew that a British assault against his capital was inevitable—the only question was when. As it turned out, he had plenty of time to reinforce his garrison and prepare his defences.

Over the winter of 1757–58, the new British prime minister, William Pitt the Elder, convinced a reluctant King George II to eliminate the French from North America. As a first step in achieving that goal, General James Abercrombie arrived on December 30 to replace the ineffectual Lord Loudoun. On February 19, 1758, Major General Jeffrey Amherst followed with additional troops—and instructions to capture Louisbourg. Amherst was successful and Governor Drucourt surrendered the strongest fortress ever constructed in North America on July 27.

The terms of surrender included giving up all claims to Île Royale and Île Saint-Jean forever. With Louisbourg out of the way, the path lay open to a far richer prize and the very heart of New France—Quebec. To ensure that Louisbourg would never again be a threat to British power, the soldiers and sailors loaded its cut and dressed stones onto ships and sent them to Halifax, where the capital's wealthy citizens used them in building their houses.

New France Falls

Other British successes followed further inland before the great British victory on the Battle of the Plains of Abraham on September 13. A year later, the British advanced on Montreal, which surrendered on September 8, forever ending French power in Canada. Although the fighting in North America was over, it took until 1762 for the Seven Years' War to end in Europe, India, and the West Indies, with Britain and Prussia victorious. By the Treaty of Paris, signed in 1763, France

The Cape Breton council in 1784

→

be called. One problem was with the colony's citizens. As the vast majority were French-speaking Acadians or Gaelic-speaking Scots, they did not meet the requirement of being able to speak English to vote or run. Both groups were also precluded for being Roman Catholic. As well, authorities deemed the island too poor to support an assembly.

The king's instructions prohibited the authorities from taking any action or passing any laws that affected the life and liberty of the island's residents, or imposed a duty or a tax. In 1816, a duty on alcohol imposed by the governor and council was challenged and the courts had no choice but to invalidate it. The colonial secretary, Lord Bathurst, decided that a representative body necessary to make such taxation legal would adversely affect the limited prosperity that Cape Breton then enjoyed, and that there were not enough people "in easy circumstances" to constitute an assembly. His only choice was to reconstitute the island as a part of Nova Scotia.

Joseph Frederick Wallet DesBarres, governor of Cape Breton from 1784 to 1787

renounced all claims to Nova Scotia (which included present-day New Brunswick and Prince Edward Island), New France, the Ohio Valley, and all territory east of the Mississippi, except for New Orleans. France was allowed to retain two small islands in the Gulf of Saint Lawrence off Newfoundland—Saint-Pierre and Miquelon—as fishing stations; they remain French possessions today.

Initially, Nova Scotia gained considerable territory from the war. On October 7, 1763, a proclamation annexed Cape Breton and Saint John's (Prince Edward) islands to peninsular Nova Scotia. The annexations were short-lived, however. Saint John's Island became a separate colony in 1769, the result of agitation caused by its absentee landlords. Initially,

Cape Breton became a county of Nova Scotia, but in 1784 it too became a distinct entity like Saint John's Island. Cape Breton had its own governor and council until 1820, when it was re-annexed to the mainland.

New England Planters

The Expulsion of the Acadians and the later arrival of the Loyalists are seminal events in the history of Nova Scotia, both having changed the human face of the province. In between these two great upheavals—neither of which was voluntary—there occurred another major movement of people, one undertaken freely. The arrival of the New England Planters (an old term for a farmer or a settler on forfeited lands) has been eclipsed by the two tragedies, but arguably had as great an influence on the young colony.

To address the continuing dearth of British

Needless to say, Lord Bathurst's decision was universally condemned by Cape Bretoners. For the next quarter century, the assembly at Halifax heard a continuous stream of complaints about the neglect of the island and its interests. In any case, none of Bathurst's successors could be convinced to overturn his decision and a legal objection to the re-annexation mounted by Cape Bretoners was eventually rejected by the Judicial Committee of the Privy Council. Despite this judgment, some Cape Bretoners remain convinced today that separation from mainland Nova Scotia would be a panacea for the island's economic ills.

A view of Sydney on Cape Breton Island in the 1700s

settlers in the province, the government tried to entice New Englanders to come to Nova Scotia and take up free grants on the vacated lands, which the Acadians had so painstakingly prepared and tilled for years. The main New England immigration occurred between 1760 and 1765. It gave the colony a decidedly New England air and had the potential—unsuspected at the time—to cause problems for the government during the American Revolution a few years later.

Even though the British conquered the French, they continued to deport the Acadians until 1763, by which time about three-quarters of Nova Scotia's Acadians had been sent away. A major problem was finding enough people who were loyal to the Crown to resettle in the colony. Several of the Thirteen Colonies to the south along the eastern seaboard were well populated—perhaps even overpopulated in the case of many parts of New England—and consisted of people who had already experienced the rigours of establishing themselves on the frontier. There was not much room left for expansion in New England after 120 years of settlement, and most of the best land was already taken. Additionally, the British issued a ruling forbidding New Englanders from settling on native hunting grounds west of the Appalachians in an attempt to keep peace with the natives.

In 1758, the Board of Trade directed Governor Charles Lawrence to distribute a physical description of the land in Nova Scotia to New Englanders. On October 12, ten days after the first assembly convened, Lawrence published a description of the vacant Acadian lands and asked for proposals for their settlement in the *Boston Gazette*. Questions followed from interested individuals, and Lawrence answered these in a second proclamation published in the *Gazette* on January 11, 1759.

The terms of settlement were quite attractive. Townships would be established of 40,500 hectares (100,000 acres). Within each township, settlers could receive a maximum of 405 hectares (1,000 acres), based on their ability to enclose and cultivate it. Each family head was entitled to a minimum of 40.5 hectares (100 acres) of woodland, plus an additional 20 hectares (50 acres) for each family member. A settler would be obliged to plant, cultivate, improve, or enclose one-third of his land every ten years for thirty years.

During the first ten years, no rent would be charged, and after that it would be at the rate of a shilling a year for every 20 hectares (50 acres). Other information concerned life in the colony, and Lawrence assured potential settlers they would feel at home in Nova Scotia. All Protestants were guaranteed freedom of religion, settlers were assured that the form of government at the local and provincial level would be "constituted in like manner with those of" New England, townships consisting of fifty families or more were entitled to send two representatives to the assembly, and each township would have a fort garrisoned by British troops.

These advertisements attracted the interest of many New Englanders, as hundreds of farmers were looking for cheap, arable land, and similar numbers of fishermen were anxious to take advantage of the productive fishery there. On April 18, 1759, representatives of prospective settlers appeared before the Council of Twelve in Halifax and were taken in an armed ship to examine potential townships in the company of Charles Morris, the province's surveyor general. The agents advised the council that they were willing to establish townships at Horton and Cornwallis on Minas Basin, and additional grants were soon issued for townships at Falmouth, Onslow, Granville, Annapolis, Cumberland, Amherst, Sackville, Tinmouth (New Dublin), Liverpool, Barrington, and Yarmouth.

Although Louisbourg had fallen, there was reluctance amongst the New Englanders to occupy these lands because some Acadians and Mi'kmaq carried on guerrilla warfare as long as Quebec remained French. Due to attacks at Cape Sable, Lunenburg, Dartmouth, Windsor, Canso, and Sackville, the council decided that all grants issued for 1759 would not take effect until the next spring. In 1760, the New

A view of Cornwallis, Grand Pré, and Basin of Minas from Horton Mountains after the New England Planters settled there

England Planters started to arrive. Lawrence died unexpectedly shortly afterwards, on October 19, 1760, after catching a chill. Although Henry Ellis was appointed to succeed Lawrence, he never came to Nova Scotia and Chief Justice Jonathan Belcher acted in his absence, first as administrator, and then as lieutenant-governor.

The Planters brought with them the form of government that had evolved in New England, based on the township. The township was the most important part of political life, where people participated directly in democracy through town meetings and the election of local officials. This was not the same form of government the Planters found in Nova Scotia, despite Lawrence's assurances in his second proclamation. Instead of the decentralization of power to the townships, the Planters faced a strong central government dominated by an oligarchy of Halifax merchants and office-holders, which wanted to increase its power. The New Englanders were only allowed to elect a few local officials, allocate land to new settlers, and administer the poor.

In 1765, this limited authority was reduced even more when the government passed "An Act for the Choice of Town Officers and regulating Townships." This measure established the form of local government in the colony for over a hundred years. The act took away the townships' right to elect local officials. Instead, it authorized the grand jury of each county to nominate two or more individuals from each township for local office, with the court of quarter sessions—controlled from Halifax—making the final decisions. In effect, the government in Halifax selected these office-holders. Two years later, the government extended its control further by taking over the responsibility for granting land in the townships. This left the townships with only the responsibility to provide for the poor.

Although some Planters protested this lack of freedom, they had little documented authority to back their claims. Invariably, they mentioned the liberties they possessed in New England—which had never been granted to Nova Scotians—and could only use the proclamation of a dead governor as the basis for asking for additional rights, which Lawrence's successors were loathe to grant.

Planters continued to arrive in Nova Scotia until 1768, when the Treaty of Fort Stanwix between the British and the Iroquois League opened up the Ohio country to them. By then, about eight thousand New Englanders had arrived in Nova Scotia; they constituted the largest single group in the province's thirteen thousand inhabitants. They established additional townships at Newport, Chester, and elsewhere. Although the Planters were the first significant English population in Canada, their presence is usually referred to in relation to another group who arrived later—the Loyalists. Today the Planters are often called the pre-Loyalists or Nova Scotia's Yankees.

By the time of the unrest that eventually became the American Revolution in 1775, almost two-thirds of Nova Scotia's inhabitants were either born in New England or children of parents born there. This make-up had the potential to create an unanticipated and dangerous situation during the Revolution, when the republican leanings of the New Englanders could sway their loyalties towards their former homes in the Thirteen Colonies, rather than to their new homes in Nova Scotia.

After the Treaty of Paris was signed in 1763, the British allowed any Acadians who agreed to sign the oath of allegiance to return to Nova Scotia—and actively encouraged it in some cases. The Acadians arrived to find New Englanders working their land, some of the best in the colony. Not wishing to see the Acadians as a possible future threat, the British scattered them across Nova Scotia, relegat-

The Honourable Michael Francklin was lieutenant-governor of Nova Scotia

ing them to remote locations on land that was largely marginal at best. The returning Acadians founded many of the current Acadian communities in the Maritimes—the west coast of Nova Scotia (known today as the French Shore), coastal Cape Breton, northern Prince Edward Island, northern and northeastern New Brunswick, and along the upper Saint John River.

The Yorkshire Immigration

Another settlement scheme, orchestrated by Lieutenant-Governor Michael Francklin, resulted in eleven groups of Yorkshire families, totalling over a thousand settlers, emigrating to Nova Scotia between 1772 to 1775. They settled on Francklin's large land holdings on the Isthmus of Chignecto, which had been largely uninhabited since the departure of the Acadians. Another fifteen percent settled in the Annapolis Valley. The arrival of Yorkshire families in a colony with a small population at the time had a major impact on many aspects of life in the province, including settlement patterns and politics. In fact, Yorkshiremen who remained loyal to the Crown played a part in preventing Nova Scotia from becoming a part of the United States during the Revolutionary War.

Chapter 6
Revolution and Rebellion

The Eddy Rebellion

TWO OF THE WAYS THAT GOVERNMENTS HAVE changed historically are through revolution and rebellion. During the American Revolution, a group of insurgents in Nova Scotia tried to do just that by encouraging a rebellion—the only one in the province's history. They wanted to make Nova Scotia the Fourteenth Colony of the new United States, joining the other thirteen in their struggle for independence from Britain.

With almost two-thirds of the population of Nova Scotia either New England–born or the children of New England parents, some people shared the attitudes of their American cousins and were sympathetic to the rebellious murmurings emanating from the Thirteen Colonies to the south. In addition, several close ties had developed over the years between New England and Nova Scotia based on trade, travel, and kin. Many felt that a natural affinity existed between the two communities.

When trouble started in the American colonies, the Friends of Liberty, a rebel group, became active throughout the province. The organizers of the First Continental Congress, a meeting of delegates from the British North American colonies to discuss and protest the punitive laws the British had passed in response the recent colonial resistance, even sent a letter to Nova Scotia inviting

1775
American Revolution begins

1776
Loyalists start to arrive; Eddy Rebellion occurs

1783
American Revolution ends

1784
New Brunswick and Cape Breton established as separate colonies

1789
French Revolution begins; religious test removed for electors

Jonathan Eddy, the leader of Nova Scotia's only rebellion

it to send representatives, and some provincial delegates actually went to Philadelphia. Nova Scotia's executive council looked on the American Revolution with alarm. The threat was real; American armies were marching on Montreal and Quebec. Once the revolution broke out in earnest, a group of rebels from neighbouring Maine attacked a fort at the mouth of the Saint John River, destroyed it, carried off spoils, and threatened other areas in the Bay of Fundy in August 1775. In response, Governor Francis Legge had the Royal Navy patrol the bay.

On December 5, 1775, the day the Americans besieged Quebec, Legge, an unpopular individual (described by one historian as "dutiful, loyal, and courageous, but...also very stupid"), declared martial law. When he attempted to call out the militia, he met with strong opposition. Nevertheless, the assembly passed two acts, one to select militia by lot and bring a fifth of them to Halifax for its defence, the other to raise taxes to cover the expenses of such actions. These acts were a disaster for the government and a windfall for the rebel sympathizers. The rebels spread the story that the governor's intention was to send the militia to fight in New England once they arrived at Halifax.

The effect was just what the rebels wanted. Many militia companies refused to assemble, especially in Cumberland County, and the tax was opposed everywhere. Many felt no one could comply with the new laws and the authorities would not be able to enforce them in any case. Legge had never visited the countryside. From his splendid isolation in Halifax, he did not realize that country folk simply could not pay the tax, nor did he understand the deleterious effect removing men from the land to help defend Halifax would have on farming.

People pleaded with Legge to withdraw the bill. The vocal New England supporters and sympathizers in Cumberland saw their chance and succeeded in organizing a petition against militia law, which was presented to the authorities. Seeing the futility of pursuing the militia acts any further—and with the arrival of additional British soldiers in the province—the governor began to suggest a compromise. In January 1776 the council suspended the two bills; the militia could remain at home and no taxes would be collected for the time being. These actions satisfied the loyal majority while at the same time stunning the rebels as they had removed the grounds for their agitation.

The American sympathizers now realized that further demonstrations against the governor and council would come to naught; their only recourse was an invasion from the Thirteen Colonies. Four members or former members of the assembly from Cumberland County—Jonathan Eddy, John Allan, Samuel Rogers, Josiah Troop—were strong advocates of the American cause and key players in the attempts to organize support throughout the Isthmus of Chignecto. Their leader was Eddy, a fifty-year-old former British Army captain who had taken part in the capture of Fort Beauséjour from the French in 1755. He later emigrated from Massachusetts in 1763, settling near Amherst.

In February 1776, Eddy travelled to the rebellious colonies and presented his plan to capture the isthmus to George Washington, who was encamped outside of Boston to direct the siege against that city. The American general was impressed by Eddy's plan, as he realized immediately its strategic importance in any broad move against the province, but he lacked the power, particularly naval, to do anything about it. Eddy returned to Nova Scotia. Meanwhile, civil law had broken down on the isthmus, with threats and accusations becoming the order of the day. Settlers pleaded for troops to be garrisoned in the area to reassure them and dishearten the rebels.

With the defeat of the British at Boston under General William

Fort Cumberland was besieged during the Eddy Rebellion

Howe and their subsequent evacuation to Halifax, Howe became the senior military commander in Nova Scotia. Inspecting the colony's defences before he returned to New England to carry on the war, Howe decided on a full garrisoning of Fort Cumberland with two hundred Royal Fencible Americans under the command of Lieutenant Colonel Joseph Goreham. These troops arrived at Fort Cumberland in early June. Meanwhile, the ever-unpopular Legge had been recalled to London to face an inquiry into his conduct. Although he was cleared and remained governor until 1782, Legge was not allowed to return to Nova Scotia.

The Loyalists were overjoyed at the arrival of the soldiers, who immediately set about restoring the neglected fort, which had been abandoned since 1768. At the same time, they were able to sell their produce to the garrison and obtain work in the restoration. A reward of two hundred pounds was put on Eddy's head, "dead or alive," and a lesser amount on the others. Behind the scenes the rebels remained active, encouraging the Fencibles to desert, many of whom did so.

When Eddy returned from the Thirteen Colonies during the summer of 1776, the situation had changed drastically. The rebels had been driven underground, many of them choosing to cease political activity altogether. After less than a month in the area, Eddy returned to America to make a final plea for assistance. Congress, heavily involved in a major military campaign, could do nothing more than urge Massachusetts to undertake appropriate operations. In September, the Massachusetts Council agreed and granted him some ammunition and rations. He would have to recruit the soldiers on his own from the eastern part of Massachusetts—present-day Maine—an area that had supported Eddy from the start.

Throughout the autumn Eddy made preparations for an attack on Fort Cumberland. He moved supplies, built up his small, rag-tag army (often through promises of profitable looting of the loyalists) to about 180 men, and scouted the land. He also spread a false rumour that reinforcements were coming from New England, causing more locals to join him, including a few disgruntled Mi'kmaq and Acadians.

The Siege of Fort Cumberland

Several loyalists tried to rally to the fort and about a dozen local militia members succeeded. They brought the garrison's strength to some two hundred men capable of fighting, plus another two hundred women and children. Besieged, Goreham decided that his best course of action was to wait the rebels out until he was able to warn his superiors of the situation and reinforcements could be sent. Once enough additional soldiers arrived, he planned to attack Eddy.

By early November and the second week of the siege, Eddy knew that he had to take action against the fort before it was reinforced or his supporters began to slip away. Goreham quickly rebuffed an ultimatum for the garrison's surrender and prepared to be attacked. Two days later Eddy attacked in the pre-dawn darkness, but was beaten back. Unknown to Goreham, word of the garrison's plight had been received in Halifax and reinforcements were on their way.

After much discussion the rebels decided to attempt to burn the fort down in another night attack. They succeeded in setting many of the fort's buildings ablaze but did not press home their attack. The next night, with their options rapidly dwindling, the rebels attempted to fire the fort again but made no effort to attack. With the garrison still standing firm, Eddy knew that he had to take decisive action quickly. Many of the rebels had lost the stomach for a fight and concentrated on plundering or settling old scores. Starving out the fort seemed to

Eddy his only option. A raid in the early morning fog in an attempt to steal the garrison's cattle ended in several rebels either killed or wounded, their heaviest losses of the siege.

Later that morning, a Royal Navy warship carrying reinforcements arrived. Lieutenant Colonel Goreham immediately prepared to attack the rebel camp. At five o'clock Friday morning, November 29, the attacking force set off from the fort towards the rebel encampment. Catching the rebels almost completely by surprise, the main assault was over in a matter of minutes, although Eddy and some of the others escaped.

In a running battle marked by several skirmishes the soldiers pursued the rebels for ten kilometres, burning the houses, barns, and crops of anyone who was suspected of supporting the insurgents along the way. The next day a conditional pardon was offered to all rebels, less the ringleaders, resulting in about a hundred of them surrendering. Many others fled to the United States, including Eddy and other leaders. Nova Scotia's brief flirtation with rebellion was over. A violent attempt at bringing democracy to the colony instantly had failed. Eventually, democracy would arrive by more peaceful—and much more gradual—means.

During most of the American Revolution, three naval officers acted as lieutenant-governors in succession during Governor Francis Legge's enforced absence between 1776 and 1782. Mariot Arbuthnot, Sir Richard Hughes, and Sir Andrew Snape Hamond generally concerned themselves more with military matters than with governing the colony. As a result, the oligarchy of Halifax merchants and office-holders that made up the council had their own way in running the province more than they normally did.

The Loyalists Arrive

The greatest consequence of the American Revolution in Nova Scotia was the coming of the Loyalists, the residents of the Thirteen Colonies who remained loyal to the Crown and left their homes to begin new lives elsewhere. They brought with them

towards America's relationship with Britain. The whole period during which a revolutionary ideology was developed simply passed them by, compounded by Nova Scotia's remoteness, sparse settlement, and non-homogeneous population.

Halifax as viewed from the south, 1780

A fanciful view of the coming of the Loyalists in 1783

different attitudes towards government and different ideas of governing, which had a profound and lasting effect on the colony. Some of these advanced the role of the people in governing the province, while others actually retarded it. Although their loyalty to the Crown was without question, as former American colonists with a tradition of self-government, they still retained, at least in the mind of one Nova Scotian official, a "cursed republican, town-meeting spirit" that needed to be "checked by some stricter form of government."

The first large movement of Loyalists to Nova Scotia occurred barely after the war started, when the British evacuated Boston in 1776 and brought nine hundred refugees with them to Halifax. By 1783, this first trickle had swelled to a raging torrent totalling more than 34,000, including 3,500 blacks. A group of 14,000 Loyalists disembarked at the mouth of the Saint John River, 12,500 landed at Halifax, and another 8,000 waded ashore at Shelburne. For the first time in the province's history, English-speaking Protestants outnumbered French-speaking Catholics.

Due to the actual influx of Loyalists to the Saint John River valley, and an expected one to Cape Breton Island, the British government created two new colonies in 1784—New Brunswick and Cape Breton Island. New Brunswick remained permanently separated from Nova Scotia, but Cape Breton only lasted 36 years, rejoining Nova Scotia in 1820.

Some twenty thousand Loyalists remained in a much-reduced

Nova Scotia, equal to the pre-Loyalist population. Lieutenant Colonel John Parr, who succeeded to the appointment in 1782, was the governor at the time of the arrival of the Loyalists. His appointment was permanently downgraded to lieutenant-governor in 1786, a position that he held for another five years, until 1791.

Theoretically, a lieutenant-governor was subordinate to a governor-in-chief or governor general, but in reality the change in title made little difference to Nova Scotia. In 1786, a governor-in-chief was established in Quebec over all of the colonies of British North America, except for Newfoundland. Each of the colonies (Nova Scotia, New Brunswick, Prince Edward Island, and Cape Breton) now had a lieutenant-governor as the senior representative of the sovereign. Unfortunately, the governor-in-chief was virtually unreachable for much of the year when the Gulf of Saint Lawrence and Saint Lawrence River were ice bound, making communication with London much easier than with Quebec. In Nova Scotia, the lieutenant-governor continued to deal directly with the Colonial Office in London on most matters.

From the moment of their arrival, the Loyalists swamped Parr with pleas for government appointments and grants of good land in an attempt to build political power. As they saw it, their loyalty to the Crown entitled them to be given jobs, even at the expense of current incumbents. Many of the appeals were more in the form of a demand than a request. Generally, the Loyalists came from colonies with much more mature assemblies than Nova Scotia's, which usu-

Loyalists draw lots for their lands, 1784

Rose Fortune (circa 1774–1864) came to Annapolis Royal with her Loyalist parents

ally had greater powers. They were also from colonies where governors were elected by the people, and were unused to a system where governors were appointed representatives of the sovereign and not subject to removal by the people.

When the Loyalists' demands were not met as quickly as they deemed appropriate, they denounced Parr, the executive council, and the legislative assembly. Their aim was simple: they wanted to dominate both the council and the assembly. Additionally, they wanted to achieve as great a measure of local autonomy as possible, something that the earlier Planters—coming from the same town-meeting tradition—had failed to obtain.

Initially some Loyalists even thought the members of the legislative assembly were appointed for life. They soon learned this was not the case, and changed the face of government in Nova Scotia, although nearly not as quickly nor as thoroughly as they would have liked. The increased population prompted the creation four new ridings and a consequent increase in the number of seats in the assembly in 1784. Digby and Shelburne townships, and Shelburne and Sydney counties, were created out of other counties, while Cumberland and Sackville townships were absorbed into counties, making a total of nine counties and eighteen townships. This increased the number of assembly seats from thirty-six to thirty-nine, a number that remained unchanged until 1819.

The Fifth Assembly (1770–85) was known as the "Long Parliament" because it sat for fifteen years, the longest in provincial history. Basically, the various governors during this period decided not to call an election because they could not be assured of facing a new assembly any more in tune with their desires than the previous one. In the first election for the enlarged assembly after the dissolution of the Long Parliament, Loyalists took thirteen seats and one of their number, Sampson Salter Blowers, a former solicitor general of New York, was elected speaker. In some ridings, the contest had quickly developed into a conflict between pre-Loyalists and newcomers.

A black woodcutter at Shelburne

Sir John Wentworth

One of the leading Loyalists was the former royal governor of New Hampshire, John Wentworth, who desperately wanted to be governor of Nova Scotia. Although he had to be satisfied initially with the appointment of surveyor general of the King's Woods, eventually Wentworth succeeded. When Lieutenant-Governor John Parr died in office in 1791, Wentworth was ready and waiting to replace him. On May 13, 1792, he became the first non-military governor of the colony.

Wentworth tended to regard oppos-

Lieutenant-Governor Sir John Wentworth had been the governor of New Hampshire before coming to Nova Scotia

Black Loyalists on a road near Bedford Basin

Windsor as viewed from Fort Edward

ition as disloyalty—perhaps the result of his New Hampshire experience—and wasted no time in changing the face of government by stacking the Council of Twelve, the bureaucracy, and other government appointments with Loyalists. Meanwhile, several more Loyalists were elected to the assembly, resulting in a Loyalist presence throughout government.

Some historians have espoused the notion that there was a Loyalist-dominated government, but in fact the Loyalists comprised less than forty percent of the assembly during this period and could have been outvoted on any single issue. Surprisingly, the division in the assembly on various issues was not usually along Loyalist/pre-Loyalist lines. What did happen was that many non-Loyalist members joined with the Loyalists to advance the powers of the elected assembly—and their own personal interests. Most divisions in the assembly were based on a split between members from Halifax and those from the hinterland, or between those who supported the government and its appointed branches and those who wanted to broaden the powers of the assembly.

Until 1787—two years into the Sixth Assembly—relations between the council and the assembly were usually harmonious. In that year, Thomas Milledge, the first representative for Digby Township and a New Jersey Loyalist and former representative in that colony's assembly,

Government House from the southwest, July 1819

presented a motion expressing dissatisfaction with the administration of justice in Nova Scotia, which passed unanimously. After that, the relationship deteriorated.

Council members, overwhelmingly from Halifax, were appointed for life largely because of their support for government policy. They usually had common commercial interests and were related by blood or marriage. They jealously guarded their prerogative and strongly favoured the status quo, ever fearful of the infringement of an elected assembly upon their powers. The growing assertiveness of the assembly after 1787 challenged and jeopardized the

GOVERNMENT HOUSE

John Wentworth and his glamourous wife, Francis, felt that the wooden house provided as their official residence did not befit their status as the colony's first couple—and besides, it was falling down. With the assembly stacked with his supporters, adherents of the so-called Court Party, in 1799 Wentworth got its members to approve a grant of £10,500 for the construction of a stone mansion more appropriate to his position.

The cornerstone of the magnificent residence was laid in 1800, and construction began later that year. During the course of its seven-year construction, the cost rose spectacularly to £30,000 because of expensive additions and changes the Wentworths made. With only sixty thousand inhabitants and a small tax base in Nova Scotia, it was an amount the province could ill afford. So anxious were the Wentworths to occupy their new residence that they took possession in 1805, two years before it was finished. Despite complaints and opposition, Government House rose slowly. Today it is a national treasure of Georgian country architecture.

Today Government House is a national architectural treasure

council's position. It characterized relations between the two bodies for the next sixty years and could be considered the beginning of the movement for reform, which culminated in the advent of responsible government in 1848.

Despite these differences, with many elected and appointed Loyalists who saw eye to eye with him on numerous issues, Wentworth was able to raise taxes to sort out the province's finances. Although the governor proclaimed the new prosperity that followed was the result of his policies, in fact it was the result of war with Revolutionary France that began in 1793. For the next twenty-two years, Nova Scotia benefitted financially from Britain's conflict with France.

Chapter 7
The Loyalist Ascendance

The French Revolution

WHILE THE LOYALISTS WERE TRYING TO establish their new lives in Nova Scotia, events were unfolding in Europe that would have a great effect on the colony's fortunes. In 1785, British Prime Minister William Pitt the Younger introduced a bill that proposed to extend the franchise by giving the vote to copyholders (those with tenancy based on documents recorded in manorial courts) whose lands were worth two pounds a year. The measure was soundly defeated and Pitt made no further attempts to change the electoral system.

While these minor reforms were being attempted in Britain, a more spectacular change was taking place in France, one that had a profound effect on English political life. Although both countries were run by the aristocracy, France was less democratic than England, and even less of its population shared in the nation's wealth. The nobles were a pampered and privileged lot who owned almost half the land, dominated the offices in government and church, and paid almost no taxes. Beneath them, a small middle class chafed at rigid class restrictions, but not enough to do anything about them. At the bottom were the lower classes, who made up the vast majority of the population and paid most of the taxes.

At the very top was an extravagant king who oversaw an inefficient

1793
War with Revolutionary France begins

1800
Napoleonic Wars begin

1812–14
War of 1812; Chesapeake blacks arrive

1815
End of Napoleonic Wars and French Revolution

1820
Cape Breton re-annexed to Nova Scotia; first Catholic elected to Nova Scotia assembly

Edward, Duke of Kent, rebuilt Halifax's defences

government. With the successful American Revolution as an example, public discontent with the system bubbled over in 1789, when the National Assembly took control of the government. It quickly moved to abolish feudalism, serfdom, special privileges, and tithes. It declared that all classes should be taxed on the basis of equality and that all men were born free and equal with certain rights, and it guaranteed religious toleration, freedom of the press, and free speech. Central to the story of the development of democracy, it proclaimed the right of every citizen to have a say in the election of officials.

During the war with Revolutionary France (1793–1802) and the Napoleonic Wars (1803–15) that followed it, money flowed into Nova Scotia from rich French and Spanish (Spain was an ally of France) ships seized in the Caribbean by privateers and Royal Navy warships. After they were taken to Halifax, the Court of Vice-Admiralty decided their fate, which usually resulted in the ships and their cargos being sold at auction.

As well as revenue from the Court of Vice-Admiralty, additional funds were provided to Nova Scotia by Britain to improve the colony's defences. By the time the War of the French Revolution began in 1793, many of Nova Scotia's fortifications had fallen into disrepair. When Prince Edward arrived in Halifax the next year as military commander for Nova Scotia, he undertook a vast rebuilding and improvement of the city's defences to counter any potential attacks by the French. He made extensive repairs to existing defences and built new batteries and fortifications. This work contributed about one hundred thousand pounds to the local economy, an enormous sum for the time.

The Beginning of Political Parties

As the eighteenth century came to a close, the first rudimentary political parties began to develop in Nova Scotia, loosely patterned on what was happening in Britain. Originally, members of the provincial assembly did not belong to any political party, because there were no formed parties in the province, or anywhere else for that matter. Each member ran on his own strengths, and voted for what he believed was best for his constituents—and

A drawing of Mi'kmaq people on a letter signed by Edward, Duke of Kent

for himself. Over time, it was only natural that members concerned with protecting or promoting the same interests—whether roads, farming, business, or other matters—would gravitate towards one another.

Although these groups were called parties, the term is a misnomer in the modern sense. They were simply loose groupings of like-minded individuals who banded together temporarily to pursue a certain course of action. They had none of the trappings of modern political parties, such as an elected leader, platform, discipline, membership rules, or recognition with the electorate.

The first of these groupings—the Country Party and the Court Party— appeared during Wentworth's later years. With an increase in members from outside the capital as the province's hinterland became settled, the country representatives soon comprised a majority in the assembly, where they were known as the Country Party. Its members espoused country interests, such as large road and bridge grants. It was generally unsympathetic to Halifax concerns, especially those of the merchants, who wanted to reduce excise and impost duties and, by extension, the amount of money available for roads. The Country Party was known for practising economy and defending the constitutional rights of the assembly and tended to support anti-council, anti-Wentworth motions.

The Country Party was usually united in opposition to the Court

Party, which consisted of Halifax merchants and others who backed Wentworth. It supported the interests of the oligarchy of Halifax merchants and office-holders, and backed most proposals that increased their already considerable power. The Court Party was quite prepared to vote money for Halifax's good, but was unconcerned with what happened in the rest of the province.

The informal leader of the Country Party was William Cottnam Tonge, a pre-Loyalist assemblyman for Hants County. Tonge had inherited the appointment of provincial naval officer from his father, Winckworth Tonge. Wentworth tried unsuccessfully to have the younger Tonge removed as naval officer, initiating a dispute between them that lasted for several years and spilled over into other areas of provincial life. Their personal feud, in which Wentworth was particularly vindictive, reflected a greater constitutional struggle between the two parties for control of revenue and money bills. Where the country members wanted to build new roads, the court members voted more and more monies to cover the mounting costs of Government House.

Another grouping, which was known as the Church and State Party, also made its appearance in the council. Its members showed a clear regard for the policies espoused in Britain by the church and the state. They objected to the public funding of schools that did not have the Church of England as a foundation. The attitude of council members towards the established church and their religious favouritism formed an important part of what later became the reform movement's criticism of the council.

Generally, however, the assembly and council remained without true political parties for many years, partly due to the skills of successive governors after the fractious Wentworth, a group of men who ensured that no executive measure could generate a united opposition. The first genuine political parties did not appear in Nova Scotia until the election of 1836, when the Tories (Conservatives) battled the Reformers (Liberals).

Before that happened, Wentworth, imbued with notions of power as the sovereign's representative, grew more despotic as he grew older. He unwisely picked fights that he could not win with the assembly and lost complete control of money bills to it. Tonge continued to oppose him at every turn, joined by a newcomer to the assembly, Richard John Uniacke.

Wentworth versus Uniacke

Richard John Uniacke was a lawyer who later entered politics and held several key posts

Uniacke, who had fought on the side of the rebels during the Eddy Rebellion but later turned against his colleagues, practised law in Halifax and by 1800 possessed the biggest law firm in Nova Scotia. After serving as the province's solicitor general and attorney general, he became speaker of the assembly in 1799. He and Tonge, who became speaker during Uniacke's trip to England in 1805, made a formidable pair against Wentworth.

Matters came to a head after the 1806 election. Adopting a course never used in Nova Scotia and only rarely in Britain, Wentworth refused the assembly's choice of Tonge as speaker and Lewis Wilkins became speaker instead. Additionally, when the son-in-law of one of Wentworth's Loyalist friends won the most votes in Annapolis Township, the assembly found him guilty of bribery and declared his seat vacant.

In line with British parliamentary precedence, the assembly asked Wentworth for a new election writ and refused to explain why the election had been nullified. To have given the governor the reason would have presumed that Wentworth had the right to decide whether the assembly's request was valid or not—a right that he did not possess. The governor refused to issue the writ and referred the matter to

Britain for adjudication on the council's recommendation.

Uniacke argued the case on behalf of the assembly. He claimed that if a governor used his instructions from the sovereign to limit the rights of an elected assembly, then it was an illegal abuse of power. The rights of the assembly were governed only by the law and constitution of Parliament, the institution that had the exclusive right of deciding disputed elections for more than two hundred years. Uniacke argued that Nova Scotia's assembly had exactly the same right—and he won.

It was a momentous decision in Nova Scotia's struggle for democracy, as important in its own right as the earlier British decision directing Governor Charles Lawrence to call an assembly. The colony had received positive affirmation that it was fully entitled to the rights and liberties that British citizens enjoyed, something that successive governors had tried to suppress.

For Wentworth, it was a humiliating setback. Never magnanimous in defeat, he spitefully dismissed Tonge as the provincial naval officer in February 1807 for persisting in "very disrespectful and pernicious opposition to His Majesty's Government." In the end, Tonge was able to get back at Wentworth. In 1808, he was one of the first to learn that Lieutenant General Sir George Prevost had arrived unexpectedly in Halifax to replace the governor, who was at Prince's Lodge in Bedford. Tonge quickly rode out to Prince Edward's estate and had the satisfaction of being the first to tell Wentworth he was out of a job.

The governor and his wife, Frances, returned to England, where she died in 1813. Wentworth came back to Halifax to escape his creditors. When he died in 1820, he was buried beneath Saint Paul's Church, among several other of the colony's worthies. Once Prevost was installed as governor in 1808, Uniacke joined the council, still complaining that Wentworth's appointments of Loyalists had resulted in a "lamentable tendency to reduce and weaken the government."

War of 1812

The British government's decision to replace Wentworth—a civilian governor—was made easier by the Napoleonic Wars and the worsening relations with the United States. Under these conditions, it made sense to install a military governor, and Prevost, who had experience as governor of the West Indies island of Saint Lucia, was chosen. Shortly after his arrival, Prevost left the province temporarily to fight against the French in the West Indies. In his absence, the responsibility for administration fell on Judge Alexander Croke of the Court of Vice-Admiralty, "an able tho' rather unpopular character," in Prevost's words. Although Chief Justice Blowers was next in precedence to the governor, he was barred from acting as governor due to a regulation that had existed since Chief Justice Belcher had been replaced as lieutenant-governor in 1763 due to incompetence.

Sir George Prevost, lieutenant-governor of Nova Scotia

Croke promptly got into a fight with the assembly by refusing assent to an appropriation bill, which set aside money from the budget for specific purposes. In explaining his actions to Secretary of State Castlereagh, he also espoused reactionary ideas. He soon found himself in an embarrassing situation when he was unable to spend money because he had denied the appropriation bill.

When Prevost returned from his successful expedition to the West Indies, he quickly smoothed over the difficulties Croke had created with the assembly. But the spiteful Croke absented himself from the Council of Twelve for several months and demanded half his judge's salary for the time he had been acting governor, despite having received the full governor's salary during the period. British authorities rejected his claim. Prevost had the last shot by recommending that either the

PROVINCE HOUSE

During Halifax's first summer, Governor Cornwallis and his staff occupied a one-storey wooden building on the site of today's legislature. A few years later a larger building was constructed, which served as the governor's residence for another fifty years. Governor Wentworth convinced the legislature to build him a finer residence on a site set aside for a permanent legislature three blocks to the south.

The assembly met in the courthouse until 1765, when it moved into a building at the corner of Barrington and Sackville streets, and then into rented quarters on Hollis Street. Once Wentworth moved into Government House, he indicated that his former residence could be torn down and a new legislature erected there. Due to the unforeseen costs of the governor's dwelling, the assembly delayed any decision until 1811. In his Throne Speech of that year, Prevost spoke of the need for a new government building in line with "the prosperous state of the Province."

A perspective view of Province House, 1819

stipulation preventing the chief justice from administering the colony be removed, or that it also apply to the judge of the Court of Vice-Admiralty.

In 1811, Prevost became governor general and left for Quebec. Croke again became the colony's administrator. To the great relief of many, the legislature was not in session and Sir John Coape Sherbrooke—another military man—arrived to replace Prevost within two months. During Sherbrooke's time, the assembly's control of the appropriations grew, especially the road monies. Then the outbreak of war in June 1812 between Britain and the United States put a different perspective on public expenditures.

The assembly quickly voted funds to place the province "in a respectable state of defence": twenty-two thousand pounds for the militia and eight thousand for blockhouses and arming boats, as well as approval for borrowing up to twenty thousand pounds (as Sherbrooke needed it) and the issue of twelve thousand pounds in treasury notes. The money for these outlays was raised by imposing additional duties on liquor: sixpence a gallon on wines, fourpence a gallon on rum, and sixpence on all other spirits. During the second year of the War of 1812, the assembly voted an additional fifty thousand pounds for defence that the governor had requested. But it continued to jealously guard the road monies. The assemblymen only partially accepted Sherbrooke's recommendation not to divide the road allowance into penny packets so small that the work of one year was "scarcely perceptible on the return of another."

The booming trade that the war brought to Halifax resulted in an increase in government revenues and in 1814 the legislature voted £15,000 for roads and bridges, the most to date. The next year this rose to £24,950. Sherbrooke, ever mindful of the need to improve the major roads in the province, again stressed the importance of allocating some funds to them. Flush with cash, the assembly partially acceded to his wishes and voted £5,000 for the main thoroughfares, leaving the rest to be doled out to road commissioners across the colony—men nominated by assembly members. As one of the few important financial expenditures the assembly actually controlled, the allocation of money to roads continued to be one of the main items it considered for many

A modern photo of the upper staircase in Province House

Lieutenant General Sir John Coape Sherbrooke, lieutenant-governor of Nova Scotia

HMS Shannon leading her prize, the American frigate Chesapeake, into Halifax Harbour on June 6, 1813, during the War of 1812

years. Frequently, the annual apportionment of these funds took up an inordinate amount of the assembly's time.

The Black Refugees

Besides an increase in revenues, the War of 1812 also brought additional people to the province. Soldiers and sailors swaggered along Halifax's streets, transients—hoping to make a fast buck—thronged to the city, and black slaves from the Chesapeake Bay area—enticed to come over to the British side with a promise of freedom and a better way of life—arrived aboard Royal Navy warships. In February 1815, Sherbrooke asked the assembly to help the black refugees and "make provision for the assistance of the distressed among these people, and to facilitate the settlement of the residue upon the forest lands of the Province."

It took until April before Sherbrooke's request was answered. In the end, the assemblymen voted a miserly five hundred pounds, despite the colony's coffers being flush with cash. The assembly also noted, reflecting a prejudice typical of the time, that they "observe with concern, and alarm, the frequent arrival in this province of Bodies of Negroes, and Mulattoes, of whom many have already become burdensome to the public."

The assemblymen claimed they were "unwilling by any aid of ours to encourage the bringing of Settlers in this Province, whose character, principles and habits, [were] not previously ascertained." The members suggested that

> the proportions of Africans already in this country is productive of many inconveniences; and that the introduction of more must tend to the discouragement of white labourers and servants, as well as to the establishment of a separate and marked class of people, unfitted by nature to this climate, or to an association with the rest of His majesty's Colonists.

In view of these concerns, they asked Sherbrooke "to prohibit the bringing any more of these people, into this Colony."

The refugees suffered for several years, due to a combination of climate, poor food, and sickness. Eventually, many of them were dispersed to various parts of the province and given land. Several of them settled at Preston, east of Halifax, which was the site of previous settlements by Black Loyalists and Jamaican Maroons. Many of these earlier arrivals departed for Sierra Leone, a colony the English had founded a few years earlier as a place where slaves who were brought to Britain and subsequently freed—or who fought on the British side during the American Revolution—could be repatriated to Africa.

The property of those who left reverted to the Crown, leaving enough room at Preston for two hundred families in a settlement favourable for agriculture.

Sadly, many of the plots allocated to the blacks were on marginal land for farming, making it impossible for many of them to sustain themselves, and they continued to rely on government support for several years. For most of the nineteenth century, the only involvement of the province's black population in politics was at election time, when candidates of all stripes tried to buy their votes. For the rest of the time, they were largely ignored.

A Period of Harmony

Along with black refugees, the end of the war saw the start of a new wave of several thousand immigrants, many from Scotland and Ireland. Sherbrooke left Nova Scotia in 1816 to become governor general, replacing Sir George Prevost, who was in disgrace because of his poor performance at one of the last battles of the war near Plattsburg, New York. Sherbrooke's relations with the assembly had been harmonious, perhaps in part because wartime concerns focused attentions elsewhere. His successor was George Ramsay, Earl of Dalhousie.

Dalhousie did not have the concerns that some of his predecessors did over the fund-

SHIP NEWS

Saturday eve. Aug. 27 arr. sch New-Providence, 54 days from BORDEAUX; sch Union, 10 days from Bay Chaleur; brig Christian, Henrick, from Newport for Amelia island, sent in by one of H. M. cruisers for a breach of blockade; brigs Resolution, and Lapwing from St. Johns, N. F.; sloop Polly, sent in by the Liverpool Packet. *Sailed* H. M. Packet, Princess Mary, for Falmouth.

Sunday, Aug. 28.—Arr. H. M. sch. Lawrence, from Canso; brig Princess Royal, 14 days from Quebec; ship Hannah, from do; sch. Edward, do; brig Brothers, 6 days from Sydney. *Sailed,* H. M. S. Dather Capt. Henderson, on a cruize.

Monday, Aug. 29—arr. ship Halifax Packet, Capt. Richards, 43 days from Cork, sailed with a fleet for this place and Newfoundland, under convoy of H. M. ships Newcastle, of 50 guns, Lord Geo Steuart, Captain, and Antelope, 50 guns, S. Butcher, Esq. Captain.

Passengers in the Halifax Packet—Doctor and Mrs. SUTHER.

Tuesday, Aug. 30.—Arr. brig Sykes, from Cork.

Wednesday, Aug 31.—Arr. brig Commerce, Capt. Tait, 16 days from Quebec; American privateer brig Ida, of 10 guns and 65 men. She was captured 9th inst. by H. M. S. Newcastle, after a chace of 12 hours, during which she threw over 8 of her guns; she was pierced for 20. The Ida, captured during her cruize, ship Hero, from Burin, N. F. for the Mediteranian, (arrived in the U. S.;) also, captured, plundered and burnt ship Alexander, from Mirimachie bound to Ayr, and sch. Francis, from Newfoundland.

Thursday, Sept. 1—arr. H. M. brig Jaseur, Capt Watt, 10 days from the Chesapeake; also, a Transport with a *few* hundred Negroes (dead and alive); sch Joseph & Polly, 8 days from St Andrews; sch Elizy-Ann, Trask, 10 days from St Johns, N. F.; H. M. brig Dotterell, from New-Providence, long passage; Portuguese ship ——, from St Salvador, for New London, sent in by H. M ship Saturn.

Friday, Sept 2—arr. H. M. cutter Landrail, of 4 12-lb. carronades, re-captured from the Americans off Cape Sable, on the 28th ult. by the Wasp brig, Capt Crawford.

The "Ship News" section of the *Acadian Recorder* reported the arrival of "a few hundred Negroes (dead and alive)" from the *Chesapeake* at Halifax on September 1, 1814

ing for roads. In his view, it was only natural that "a little self interest and private friendship" on the part of the assemblymen was a consideration in the distribution of such monies. Having had its point of view accepted for road funding, the assembly also began to assert itself in other various ways; upholding the privileges of its members, rejecting the council's proposed agent in London, and refusing to split a bill incorporating various bounties into three separate bills, as the Council of Twelve had demanded.

George Ramsay, 9th Earl of Dalhousie

The prosperity that the War of 1812 brought to Halifax continued for a few years after the war ended. Then, as happened before—and would happen again—a post-war recession hit the colony, with the initial signs appearing during Dalhousie's time. One of the first items that got reduced was road funding. In the new session of 1819, Dalhousie proposed various improvements to agriculture (a personal interest of his), a college in Halifax, changes to the militia, and a new system of building roads. Any increases to make up revenue shortfalls to pay for these changes he believed could come from an increase in duties. Although Dalhousie failed to get approval for changes to the militia and control of road improvements, he did get approval for a college and support to agriculture.

Towards the end of 1819, Dalhousie learned that he was to follow in the footsteps of Prevost and Sherbrooke and become governor general. Due to the lateness of the season, he decided to remain in Halifax and opened the session of 1820. Provincial revenues had continued to decline, resulting in only ten thousand pounds being allocated for roads, down from a high of twenty-five thousand in 1817. Then, when unofficial word of the death of King George III came on March 27, the session hastened through a number of items, believing that once the word was received officially the session would end.

Although Dalhousie displayed an affable front to the assembly and council, his private thoughts were very different. He confided to his diary that the assemblymen were "petulant and grasping at more than their privileges; they do not abide by the rules of Parliament... they throw aside all regularity and order of proceeding...Incredibly ignorant and too much self-interested." He described the speaker as "an ill-tempered crab, deeply tinctured in Yankee principles...an unfit person to be the Speaker."

When he learned that the assembly had not responded to certain specific questions and proposals he had put to them earlier, Dalhousie became extremely perturbed. He turned down the award of a ceremonial sword and a star-shaped medal or decoration for which the assembly had previously voted one thousand guineas, even though he had initially accepted them. The assemblymen were shocked, and wondered at the lieutenant-governor's "inconsistent and absurd" action. If Dalhousie's temperament was sorely tested by the easygoing assemblymen of Nova Scotia, they thought there was little hope of him dealing effectively with their much more aggressive colleagues in Lower Canada.

Major General Sir James Kempt replaced Dalhousie as lieutenant-governor, and proved to be a calming influence. He carefully scouted out the terrain on both sides of the ocean before any potentially con-tentious matters came to a head, conscious of the effect that any new legislation that might be proposed would have on Nova Scotia. One of his first official actions was the re-annexation of Cape Breton in October 1820.

An important political debate at the time revolved around the status of Roman Catholics. Laurence Kavanagh, a Catholic elected to the assembly in 1820, was prepared to take the oath of allegiance to the Crown, but not those oaths required by British law against popery (an offensive term

An 1823 election cartoon entitled "Electioneering against Johnny Bluenose"

referring to the Roman Catholic Church, its doctrines, or its practices) and the doctrine of transubstantiation (the transformation of the bread and wine of Communion into the body and blood of Jesus Christ in substance, but not appearance, during the Mass). After discussion between the assembly, council, and lieutenant-governor, as well the involvement of Colonial Secretary Lord Bathurst, Kavanagh was allowed to become an assemblyman after taking only the state oaths.

In the 1827 session of the assembly, humorist Thomas Chandler Haliburton, a newly elected member, raised the subject of Catholics, leading the assembly in demanding the total removal of oaths against popery and transubstantiation. "Who," he demanded, "created the magna carta? Who established judges, trial by jury, magistrates, sheriffs, etc? Catholics! To that calumniated people we were indebted for all that we most boasted

FIRST ROMAN CATHOLIC MEMBER OF THE ASSEMBLY

Laurence Kavanagh was born in Cape Breton in 1764 of parents who had emigrated to Nova Scotia from Waterford, Ireland, in 1760. He was a fish and shipping merchant and in 1820 was elected as one of the first two members for Cape Breton County, along with Richard John Uniacke (the son of the Richard John Uniacke of Lieutenant-Governor John Wentworth's time). Due to the delay in getting permission from Britain for Kavanagh to become a member of the assembly, he did not take his seat until April 3, 1823, becoming the first Catholic to do so.

Kavanagh served until his death in 1830. His place was taken by his son, also named Laurence Kavanagh, who ran as a Reformer in the election that immediately followed his father's death. The son was member for Cape Breton County from 1830–36. In 1836, he was elected as the first member for Richmond County, and served until 1840. He became the second Roman Catholic to sit in the House of Assembly, although Lawrence Connor Doyle (elected 1832) has often been credited with that distinction.

Lieutenant-Governor Sir James Kempt

of." His equally new colleague historian Beamish Murdoch declared Haliburton's outburst "the most splendid piece of declamation that it has ever been my fortune to listen to."

By the middle of the 1820s, the economic situation in the province began to recover from its post-war slump, and road allowances increased to twelve thousand pounds in 1824. In April, Kempt left for England on private business and Michael Wallace, the senior councillor, became administrator in his absence. Perhaps mindful of the tumultuous administration of Alexander Croke when the province had been temporarily without a lieutenant-governor earlier, Wallace refrained from any controversial action.

Kempt's last session was in 1828, before he went to Quebec as successor to Dalhousie, who was experiencing difficulties with Louis-Joseph Papineau and his colleagues in the Lower Canada Assembly. Before he departed, Kempt made a final attempt to change the way the road grants were administered, but the assembly agreed to only one of his two proposals, concerning the province's great (main) roads. The country assemblymen were still not prepared to give up their control of funds for maintaining the colony's cross (secondary) roads.

During his time as lieutenant-governor, Kempt's relationship with the assembly had been perhaps the most harmonious in the province's history. He was aided in this by the twenty-year-old system of voting supplies (money for the cost of government), which the country assemblymen supported, as well as by the leading members of the assembly, who conducted articulate debates on many subjects, but never questioned the system of government itself. But that was about to change very shortly, spurred on by the reform movement in Britain.

Chapter 8
Reform Begins

Problems with the Executive Council

IN MANY WAYS IT WAS THE ACTIONS AND COMPOSITION of the executive council in Nova Scotia that led to the growth of the reform movement in the province, an idea that originated in Britain. Traditionally, members of the Council of Twelve were appointed for life, which led to many absences due to old age and illness. This frequently resulted in a delay in government business because a quorum was unavailable. Although early governors submitted lists of suitable persons to the Board of Trade for consideration as councillors, the board's own nominees usually received the appointment. In Halifax's early days, more often than not they were the candidates of Joshua Mauger, a Halifax businessman who dominated the oligarchy of Halifax merchants and office-holders, both while he lived in Halifax and on his return to England.

After the American Revolution, the nominees proposed by the governors were usually selected. Additionally, provisional appointments to the Council of Twelve were allowed, which solved the quorum problem. Because John Wentworth was governor for such a long period, this meant that the council was largely composed of his friends.

Governors faithfully selected their nominees from people who were "well disposed towards government," in accordance with

1827
Jotham Blanchard becomes editor of *Colonial Patriot* in Pictou

1829
Blanchard begins writing anti-government editorials

1830
Joseph Howe takes up reform cause in his *Novascotian* editorials; final restrictions on Catholics running for office removed

1832
Howe embarks career as a reformer; British Reform Bill passed

their instructions. In practice, this meant that every executive and administrative act of the provincial bureaucracy tended to be accepted by the council without question. The council was composed mostly of persons who held offices and received their salaries from the government. Councillors jealously guarded their positions, and generally opposed any regulation proposed by the assembly if it affected them in their official capacities in one way or another.

Gradually, more and more of the councillors—and by extension the principal office-holders in the province—were related by marriage. Although the Nova Scotia Council of Twelve never approached the magnitude of Upper Canada's Family Compact, the most outstanding example of family connections in the province was the Gerrish-Brenton-Halliburton-Stewart-Inglis-Collins-Cochran-Hill-George grouping. It provided eleven councillors, about one-fifth of all those appointed before 1830. From 1759 to 1848, a substantial part of the government was concentrated in this small group of associated families who strongly supported the status quo to preserve their happy situation.

Another weakness in the structure of the council was in its

Province House, 1830

geographical composition: it was a Halifax body, not a Nova Scotian one. Few councillors came from outside the capital city or its environs. Of the fifty-one councillors appointed in the seventy years between 1760 and 1830, a mere six were "country" folk, and none of them attended the forty or more sessions held each year with any degree of regularity.

Using the exaggeration for which he was noted, in 1827 Thomas Chandler Haliburton provided a cutting description of the councillors in the pages of the *Novascotian* newspaper:

Thomas Chandler Haliburton, author, judge, and politician

> Two thirds of them have never been beyond Sackville Bridge [just outside Halifax at the head of Bedford Basin], and think all the world is contained within the narrow precincts of Halifax. Two or three of the younger sisters indulge in a ride on the post road every summer, into the country, and have acquired the names of the villages and the inn-keepers, but that is the extent of their knowledge. They then return to town, talk sagely of roads and bridges, agriculture, rural affairs and common schools. They are looked upon as walking gazetteers, and living directories.

To be fair, some of the geographically unrepresentative nature of the Council of Twelve was due to the requirement for the council to be able to quickly establish a quorum on short notice, an impossibility if several council members had to travel a great distance, given the dearth of suitable transportation links across the province.

The Development of the Legislative Assembly

From the time it was first established in 1758—and in concert with British colonial governments elsewhere—the elected assembly grew steadily in power. Its representative nature, which had grown into a patchwork quilt lacking any sort of principles, gradually improved. On the other hand, in the early years of the assembly, it would have been impossible to have province-wide representation as the population was overwhelmingly concentrated in Halifax. Early assemblies were made up largely of Halifax men, and it was often Haligonians who represented areas outside the capital. Although not always united in their views, the Halifax representatives tended to be closely associated with the oligarchy of Halifax merchants and office-holders and jealously protected their interests.

On the rare occasions when the country members of the assembly wanted to go against the Halifax interests, there were ways of circumventing them. On one occasion, the Gerrish brothers convinced enough of their fellow assemblymen to walk out of the House, which prevented a quorum being formed to pass legislation detrimental to their own activities. Sessions could also be prolonged or adjourned, which normally put the country members in a minority.

Obtaining a quorum was difficult at the best of times and, in an effort to improve attendance, the Third Assembly voted various disciplinary measures for non-attendance in the early 1760s. Any absentees at the start of a session were summoned by courier and could be expelled unless they appeared by a certain date, while sitting members were ordered not to absent themselves unless they had the permission of the speaker. Usually, the assembly failed to enforce these measures, although the Fifth Assembly declared twenty-nine seats vacant. Generally however, such punitive measures had little effect.

Taking another tack, in 1770 the assembly reversed its earlier, long-standing position on providing remuneration to its members and directed the counties to pay any of their representatives who wanted to be paid five shillings a day, in accordance with an old English practice. When this failed to produce the desired results, the legislature decided to provide such funds itself—a procedure without English precedent. Although a few members agreed with the English opinion that any legislative body that voted monies for itself prostituted itself, far more thought otherwise and the measure passed. In 1781, the daily amount was increased to ten shillings to members who attended. Payment seemed to have the desired effect and, after 1781, the attendance of country members was no longer a problem, as the cost of their transportation, lodging, meals, and other expenses was now reimbursed, at least in part.

Another transformation in the assembly occurred with the appearance of emerging parties, notably the Country Party, made up of members from outside Halifax and its environs (including Halifax County). With an increase in members from outside the capital as the province's hinterland became settled, the country representatives soon comprised a majority in the assembly. They were usually united in opposition to the interests of the Halifax oligarchy, and deeply suspicious of any proposals that increased its already considerable power.

Reform in Britain

The ideas of the reform movement had begun in Britain before being considered in Nova Scotia. Initially, most Englishmen were content to see the events of the French Revolution unfold, especially the reformers. Once the Revolution turned into a bloodbath of the aristocracy and bourgeoisie, however, the British upper classes panicked. Thomas Paine, who had earlier urged the American colonists to revolt, now published a revolutionary book entitled *The Rights of Man.* In it, he argued that government was derived from the people and that the monarchy and the House of Lords should be abolished, to be replaced by a democratically elected House of Commons.

Many members of the upper classes were fearful of a revolution breaking out, and Parliament passed a series of repressive measures. Eventually, working class agitation died down, partly because of disenchantment over the violence of the French Revolution. The British aristocracy breathed easy again—at least for a time.

After Napoleon's defeat at Waterloo in June 1815, Britain and its institutions were not geared to the changes happening in society brought on both internally by a growth in population and the rise of industrial towns in the north, and externally by the American and French revolutions and the Napoleonic Wars. Sharper class distinctions led to bitter class antagonisms. The nobility and the landed gentry enjoyed power and prestige difficult to comprehend now. They controlled the political life of the nation, owned much of the land, ran the church, possessed pocket boroughs (where elections were controlled by a person or a family), and attended universities open only to them. The middle classes were growing in both numbers and wealth, but were still largely excluded from political power. The lower classes made up the vast majority of the country—deprived, dispossessed, disenfranchised, and desperate.

Although Britain proudly proclaimed its constitution, in reality it was a handful of landed aristocrats who governed the country—and badly, at that. While it was true that the power of the sovereign had been diminished, the monarch still influenced the composition and actions of the government. Cabinet solidarity was just developing, and most ministers acted independently, regarding themselves as servants of the king.

Reform of the House of Commons to more accurately reflect the population patterns of the country and extend the franchise was desperately needed. But any hope for reform based on the American Revolution had been dashed by the excesses of the French Revolution. No matter how necessary or slight, any proposal for reform was decried as dangerous and radical. "Democracy" became a dirty word, invoking memories of the Reign of Terror in France.

The middle classes—at least for the moment—remained detached from the movement for democratic suffrage, leaving the working classes to go it alone. Rich and poor moved farther apart, and the enmity between them grew. For its part, the cabinet—whether Tory or Whig—did everything it could to preserve the status of the upper classes, believing that any change was likely to be for the worse.

Reform Begins—Slowly

The possibility for change began to appear in 1822, when Tory Sir Robert Peel became

the Crown. After the revolution, the Tories accepted some of the Whig doctrine of a limited constitutional monarchy rather than divine-right absolutism. Tories came to represent the resistance, mainly by the country gentry, to religious tolerance and foreign entanglements. Toryism became identified with the Church of England and the country gentry, while Whiggism became associated with the aristocratic, landowning families and the financial interests of the wealthy middle classes.

The reign of George III (1760–1820) brought a shift of meaning to the two terms. Real party alignments began to take shape after 1784, when serious political issues, such as the American Revolutionary War, deeply stirred public opinion. After 1784, William Pitt the Younger emerged as the leader of a new Tory party, which broadly represented the interests of the country gentry, the merchant classes, and official administrative groups. In opposition, a revived Whig Party under Charles James Fox came

→

→

to represent the interests of religious dissenters, industrialists, and others who sought electoral and parliamentary reforms.

Although the French Revolution and the wars against republican France complicated the division between the parties, after 1815 there eventually emerged the conservatism of Sir Robert Peel and Benjamin Disraeli and the liberalism of Lord John Russell and William Gladstone, with the party labels of Conservative and Liberal assumed by the respective factions.

home secretary. A non-aristocrat, Peel was not set in his beliefs and was prepared to change them based on evidence. Despite there being liberal members in the Tory cabinet, several enlightened measures had not passed without strong opposition from ultraconservative Tories. When Prime Minister Lord Liverpool resigned for health reasons, a coalition cabinet followed, made up of both Tories and Whigs. Notably, the liberal members of both parties drew together in the new cabinet, a trend that was well-established by 1830.

When the coalition fell in 1828, it was replaced by a cabinet composed of High (right-wing) Tories. Under such a cabinet, the prospects for reform were slight. Only one measure of significant reform was passed—the Catholic Emancipation Act. This law finally allowed Roman Catholics to become Members of Parliament, a privilege they had been denied since the reign of Charles II in the seventeenth century.

By about 1830, the so-called reformers achieved some success and became more active in trying to change the way the country was governed. At the bottom of the social scale, the lower classes remained discontented and bitter, primarily due to a depression that deepened as the decade advanced. The middle class—especially its radicals—shared this discontent, believing they were not fully sharing in the nation's wealth. Protest movements and radical societies were formed to push for change.

After the general election of 1830, the Tories remained in office, with the revered Duke of Wellington, the hero of Waterloo, retained as prime minister. When he made a rash statement opposing any kind of parliamentary reform, he was replaced by Earl Grey. It marked the first time the Whigs had been in power since a brief ministry in 1806–7, and it heralded a major shift in politics.

Although Grey was described as an "aristocrat of aristocrats" who had not the slightest intention of furthering the cause of democracy, his party had a tradition of constitutional reform. As a young man, Grey had even advocated reform of the electoral system, and now he returned to his earlier theme. The fact that his cabinet consisted of mostly fellow peers gave a sense of security to the upper classes—after all, how radical could any reforms of the House of Commons be if they were instigated by the nobility?

The Reform Bill of 1832

In the summer of 1830, another revolution across the channel in France— bloodless this time—forced Charles X from the throne, to be replaced by Louis-Philippe, and established the supremacy of the middle classes. Britain quickly followed suit with the Reform Bill of 1832, which aimed to extend the franchise to the middle classes, including numerous shopkeepers. If anything, the bill was an attempt by the aristocracy to appease the middle classes, and by satisfying them, isolate the nobility and gentry from the strident demands of the lower classes.

The bill had popular support across the country, which convinced William IV to dissolve Parliament and hold an election. Such a direct appeal to the people on a single issue was unique, and the Whigs were returned with a comfortable majority. Although the Tories tried to delay the bill, it passed in the Commons and was sent to the Lords. As expected, their Lordships rejected it.

At the time, a defeat in the House of Lords was the same as a defeat in the House of Commons, normally leading to the fall of the government. But the nation wanted the bill and the people were incensed by the action of the Lords. There was a riot in Bristol and many thought a revolt would soon follow. Grey prorogued Parliament for two months to let tempers cool. When it sat again in December, the prime minister reintroduced the bill. As before, it passed in the Commons, but was stalled in the Lords.

One solution to the obstinacy of the Lords was a radical measure—the creation of enough additional peers who supported the measure to ensure its passage. Grey went to the king, demanding the creation of more peers. William refused and Grey resigned. It was a unique situation. The Commons was determined to pass the bill, and the Lords was just as determined to scupper it. When the Tories could not form a cabinet, William had to recall Grey. But the Whig would not return until the king promised to create enough new peers if it became necessary. When the Tory Lords learned that Grey possessed this power, they proceeded out of the House of Lords in a dignified procession. In their absence, the bill passed and became law in June 1832.

In reality, the Reform Bill was hardly a far-reaching measure; in modern terms, both the Tories and the Whigs would be considered conservative. It did not change the number of Commons seats, but rearranged them. In rural areas, the franchise was extended to more freeholders and tenants. In the boroughs, the hodgepodge of voting qualifications was thrown out and replaced by a universal rule that enfranchised persons who occupied residential or commercial property rated at ten pounds per year. Other parts of the bill called for a register of voters, put controls on election spending, and decreed that the polls would be open only for two days.

The importance of the Reform Bill of 1832 was not in the changes it brought to the enfranchisement of British citizens. The total electorate in the entire country only increased from 478,000 to 814,000, out of a population of around 14 million. There was still no secret ballot and all voters were subjected to the scrutiny of their superiors, which usually resulted in election day ending with a punch-up. Despite the bill, the upper classes—the landed gentry and the nobility—continued to dominate the country's political life. In fact, they were in a stronger position than before; although the irrationalities of the old way had been discarded, they did not lose any control.

Pictou as viewed from Mortimer's Point in the mid-1830s

The crucial importance of the bill was the way it was passed, which strengthened the cabinet system of government. Grey and his cabinet, supported by the House of Commons, had forced their will on the king and the House of Lords, while the Duke of Wellington, without the support of the House of Commons, had been unable to form a cabinet. Additionally, although it was not particularly liberal in itself, the Reform Bill's passage cleared the way for more liberal measures—including in Britain's North American colonies.

Reform in Nova Scotia

The progress of reform in Britain was followed closely by several Nova Scotians. Within the space of a few years, the British example led to agitation for reform in Nova Scotia, which resulted in many changes to the province's political landscape. Political parties developed, leading to the second great achievement in parliamentary democracy in the colony—the beginning of responsible government.

One of the more obscure individuals involved in the early fight against the established order was an austere Pictou County Presbyterian clergyman and independent thinker by the name of Thomas McCulloch.

Thomas McCulloch, minister and educator

McCulloch's battle with the establishment had little to do with the reform of government; it was based on his desire to create an institute of higher learning free from the requirement for its students to subscribe to the Thirty-Nine Articles of the Church of England. In 1806, McCulloch set up a school in his house with the aim of eventually training Presbyterian ministers for the province, a need previously met only by outside preachers. He hoped to establish a non-denominational university where a liberal education essential to the ministry could be obtained, but he was unable to secure government funding or permission to grant degrees.

At the time, the only institute of higher learning in the province was King's College in Windsor, founded in 1788, which effectively barred dissenters (anyone not a member of the Church of England), who made up eighty percent of the colony's population. Undaunted, McCulloch founded the Pictou Academy in 1816 and began what became his life's calling. Modelled after the Scottish academies and universities, it emphasized logical argument, scientific practices, and equality of education and opportunities.

Due to the intransigence of the majority of the Church and State Party members, the bill for the permanent support of the Presbyterian Pictou Academy never became law, and the academy survived on annual grants (McCulloch perhaps had the last laugh when he later became the first principal of Dalhousie College).

Pictou Academy was founded by Thomas McCulloch

The Forgotten Patriot of Pictou

One of the young students upon whom McCulloch had a profound influence was Jotham Blanchard, an individual who deserves far more credit for his role in the struggle for responsible government than he has received to date. As a student at the Pictou Academy, Blanchard had the ideals of more responsible government instilled in him by Thomas McCullough. He became a lawyer in 1821, and in 1827, when he was only twenty-seven, became editor of the new *Colonial Patriot*, a Pictou newspaper published by William Milne and the first in the province outside of Halifax. In April 1829, Blanchard started a weekly series that was the first to examine the detailed workings of the institutions in Nova Scotia. His editorials were the earliest printed criticisms against the Council of Twelve and for the rights of the aver-

Jotham Blanchard, the forgotten patriot of Pictou

age citizen—something that had never appeared in the Halifax newspapers. In the pages of the *Colonial Patriot*, Blanchard hinted at a change in the system of government for Nova Scotia. His writings soon came to the attention of the establishment, who viewed his opinions as radical.

Although there existed among many Nova Scotians a general feeling against the abuses of the council, there was no organ in which they could voice their concerns until the *Colonial Patriot* began publishing. Blanchard was the first to advocate responsible government in print, not only in the province, but in all of British North America. Joseph Howe, the editor of the *Novascotian* and at the time a Tory with milder opinions than other Tories, generally defended the Council of Twelve and criticized Blanchard in his newspaper, decrying him as the "Pictou Scribbler." In fact, the attacks the two editors made on each other in their newspapers actually increased their circulation.

The Brandy Dispute

Some historians assert that the practical beginnings of reform in Nova Scotia can be traced to the unilateral actions of an independently minded customs collector. In 1826, the assembly imposed a tax of one shilling and fourpence on foreign brandy imported into the province, in addition to the one-shilling tax already levied by the British government. On his own initiative, the collector of customs decided that a total of two shillings was enough duty, but neglected to inform the assembly of his actions. In 1830, Enos Collins, who was well on his way to becoming the richest man in Nova Scotia, petitioned the assembly for a refund on his customs duties, claiming that he had been given an unfair exchange rate on the Spanish doubloons with which he paid the tax. At the time, doubloons, dollars, and pounds were in circulation.

Although he didn't intend it, Collins's petition provided the assembly with the information that the customs collector was not collecting the full tax, and they immediately passed a bill to restore it. Collins (a member of the Council of Twelve since 1822) and his associates who controlled the council refused to accept the bill. For a time, no taxes at all were collected on imported alcohol and Collins took advantage of the situation by selling spirits without paying anything into the provincial treasury. His actions caused a storm in the assembly and universal outrage in the press.

Fate intervened in the form of King George IV, who died after a short ten-year reign. In accordance with British practice, the death of a sovereign required an election. The "Brandy Election" of 1830 was fought on the issue of the tax and saw almost the entire province turn on the Council of Twelve for daring to assert its power on a money bill. Jotham Blanchard ran in Pictou County and won. The election resulted in an assembly that quickly re-imposed the duty as one of its first acts. This time the council accepted its decision. Collins's actions had turned many people against him, but more importantly, they brought increased criticism of the Council of Twelve, already under attack for its high-handed ways. The cracks in the Nova Scotian political system were beginning to widen.

The next year, when Howe travelled around the province to get material for his newspaper, he discovered that many people shared Blanchard's opinions about government. In Pictou, Howe dropped in to the offices of the *Colonial Patriot* and met Blanchard. It was a fortuitous event for the future of the colony, because the Pictonian was able to convince the Haligonian of the merit of his views. As Howe later wrote, "My first education in liberal politics came at this time, and the Pictou Scribbler has converted me from the error of my ways."

Blanchard was never a very healthy man and was sickly for much of his life. Due to illness he did not run for re-election in 1836, and he died in 1839. What greater role he would have played in bringing responsible government to Nova Scotia had he lived longer cannot be determined, but it is highly likely—based on his beliefs and actions during his short life—that he would have had an important part. Fortunately, Blanchard's passion for a change in government was taken up by Joseph Howe.

CHAPTER 9
THE ACCIDENTAL REFORMER

The Road to Reform

THROUGHOUT THE 1830S AND EARLY 1840S, political reform was hotly debated in Nova Scotia, especially by people who resided outside of the capital. Halifax interests continued to control the province politically and financially, through the lieutenant-governor, the Council of Twelve, the assembly, merchants, and businessmen. Many Nova Scotians felt it was time for a change. One of them was Joseph Howe, unquestionably one of the greatest Nova Scotians who ever lived.

In 1828, when Howe became editor of the *Novascotian*, there was little of politics in the newspaper, but that soon changed and in the spring of 1829 he wrote a few political articles. The assembly had reprimanded the editors of the *Acadian Recorder* and the *Free Press* when the editors cautioned the assembly about going too far in its pursuit of John Alexander Barry. Barry, a member of the assembly, had been ordered arrested by the legislature for publishing a letter in the *Acadian Recorder* that the other members judged to be libellous. Howe sprang to his fellow editors' defence and made what was perhaps his first statement about the freedom of the press: "If Editors are brought for offences to the Bar of the House," he warned, "Legislators may depend upon this—that they will be brought, individually

1835
Howe successfully defends himself at libel trial

1836
Howe wins first election to assembly; first election with true political parties occurs; first Acadians are elected to assembly

1837
Howe proposes Twelve Resolutions; rebellions occur in Lower and Upper Canada

1838
Legislative council created

The scene of Joseph Howe's trial, the Legislative Library in Province House, which was the Supreme Court of Nova Scotia at the time

and collectively, to a bitter expiation before the bar of the public."

Joseph Howe and the Freedom of the Press

On January 1, 1835, Howe printed a letter in the *Novascotian* signed "The People" that accused the magistrates of Halifax of misconduct. It had been written by George Thompson, a friend of Howe's. Shortly after its publication, proceedings for criminal libel were instituted against Howe. The trial was scheduled for March and Howe immediately set out to find a lawyer who would defend him. When he showed two or three of them the attorney general's notice of the trial, they all advised that the case could not be successfully defended. The letter was in fact a libel, and using the defence of the truth of what had been written was not permitted in libel against a public body. Howe would have to submit to the findings of the court—likely a fine or imprisonment.

At the time there was not an incorporated city or town (one with elected representatives to govern it) anywhere in Nova Scotia. Halifax and the other municipalities were governed by magistrates, who were appointed by the Crown and were totally independent of popular control by the colony's citizens. Dissatisfaction with the magistrates was observed everywhere—especially in Halifax. People spoke of their neglect, mismanagement, and corruption. Although no one had proposed a remedy, there was certainly universal grievance against them. Howe's trial soon changed all that.

Unable to find anyone to take his case, Howe laughingly noted, "I asked them to lend me their books, gathered an armful, threw myself on a sofa, and read libel law for a week." By the end of the week, he had convinced himself that the lawyers were wrong and that there was a good defence, if only the case were presented to the court and a jury. He spent another week selecting and arranging the facts and the public documents on which his defence was based, finishing on the evening before the trial. This left him only enough time to write out

it the *Acadian*. A year later he sold his share to his partner and bought another newspaper, the *Novascotian*, for £1,050.

In July 1829, Howe began a regular series entitled "Legislative Reviews," which became very popular. Although in his earlier days he followed in his father's footsteps as a pronounced conservative, from about 1830 he championed the cause of the reformers in his newspaper, often giving offence to the prominent men of the day and making many enemies in the process. Five years later he entered fully into the public life of the province with a controversial letter printed in the *Novascotian*, and remained there until his death.

The bas-relief sculpture on the base of the statue of Joseph Howe, which depicts a scene from his famous libel trial

and commit to memory the two opening paragraphs of his speech—the rest he would have to improvise.

Howe's trial began on March 1, in what is now the Legislative Library of Province House. When Howe saw the jury, he "scarcely expected a unanimous verdict, as two or three of the jurors were connections, more or less remote, of some of the justices, but thought they would not agree" with the charge against him. The prosecuting lawyers were very civil towards Howe, but laughed at him, quoting the old maxim that "he who pleads his own case has a fool for a client." When the trial was over, Howe had the last laugh.

Howe later remarked that during his defence, "I became conscious that I was commanding the attention of the court and jury. I was much cheered when I saw the tears rolling down one old gentleman's cheek. I thought he would not convict me if he could help it." Howe's defence took more than six hours to deliver, interrupted frequently by expressions of popular feeling. Most people knew that he could write, but before now, no one—including Howe himself—realized that he possessed a wonderful orator's gift of speech.

It took the jury only ten minutes to deliberate. Breathless silence accompanied their return, but shouts of applause greeted the verdict of "Not Guilty," not only from those

BANKING AND CURRENCY PROBLEMS

Nova Scotia's first bank had been chartered in 1825 after several unsuccessful attempts when Enos Collins and a group of his merchant associates founded the Halifax Banking Company. The colony had long needed its own bank and these successful businessmen had sufficient capital to finance the new venture. Henry H. Cogswell was the company's president, but Collins was clearly the dominant partner. The bank's business was transacted in the same building that housed Collins's firm, which still exists today in Halifax's Historic Properties. Locals soon began calling the company "Collins' Bank."

Over Collins's strenuous objections, in 1832 the council granted a charter to a second bank, ending the monopoly that his bank had enjoyed for seven years. The new Bank of Nova Scotia and Collins' Bank were soon embroiled in a currency battle that weakened the colony's financial stability. Perhaps more importantly, it gave the reformers another

crammed into the small courtroom, but from the large crowds that surrounded Province House. Howe was escorted home by hundreds of ardent well-wishers, accompanied by deafening acclamations. For the rest of the day and all through the next, Haligonians of every class went on a holiday. Six weeks later, a silver pitcher arrived from New York, the gift of Nova Scotian residents in that city, and was presented to Howe in a public forum. Its inscription proclaimed "his honest independence in publicly exposing fraud, improving the morals, and correcting the errors of men in office, and his eloquent and triumphant defence in support of the freedom of the press."

Howe's successful defence of the libel suit brought against him resulted in another Canadian milestone being met in Nova Scotia—freedom of the press and, by extension, freedom of speech. Prior to Howe's victory, few newspaper editors were prepared to risk the wrath of and persecution by the governor or members of the executive council by criticizing them on the printed page. Much of what the council did—including its patronage, cronyism, and favouritism—simply went unreported. As long as the people were unaware of what was happening, there was little reason for them to complain or agitate for new and different ways of conducting the business of government. After

reason to attack the oligarchy of Halifax merchants and office-holders. The crack widened again—and Howe stepped into it.

The interrelated issues of banking and currency showed Howe the weaknesses of the assembly and council. The stringent conditions imposed on the Bank of Nova Scotia by a self-serving council, which contained five directors of the Halifax Banking Company, coupled with currency manipulations by bankers, assemblymen, and councillors that made a serious recession worse, outraged him. The year 1832 marks the beginning of Howe's career as a reformer.

A painting by C. W. Jefferys entitled "Joseph Howe after a Halifax Triumph, 1835"

Howe's victory, the public gradually became more cognizant of what the council did, leading to support for the few who had been proposing reform to make government responsible to the people.

Some people have argued that because regression occurred in both freedom of speech and the press after Howe's trial, his victory did not clearly establish these two democratic rights. For example, in December 1843, Howe's successor at the *Novascotian*, Richard Nugent, lost a series of actions for civil libel brought against him by the Tories. Unable to pay the damages the courts awarded, Nugent had to sell the newspaper and was actually imprisoned for a time. With regard to criminal libel, freedom of the press did not occur until the truth of the libel could be used as a defence. It was not until 1843 that the British Parliament enacted a statute that allowed such a defence, and then only if it could be proven that the publication of the alleged libel was for the benefit of the public.

Author and philosopher John Ralston Saul does not share the opinion of those who belittle Howe's achievement. He believes that "in the process of winning his acquittal, Howe established the fundamental ideas, principles and shapes of freedom of speech and freedom of the press in Canada," notwithstanding any later backsliding. Saul notes that the "historic link between Howe's defence and...our Charter of Rights is about as straight and clear as an historic link can possibly be."

Howe's success in his libel suit also resulted in another, lesser-known but far-reaching, achievement. Shocked by his acquittal, all the magistrates in Halifax resigned immediately. In an attempt to retain the old system, the government chose others to replace them and appointed a lawyer as a custodian to watch over them. But this last-ditch effort to retain the magistrates only lasted a few years.

In the face of continued, growing opposition to the magistrates—and with news of municipal reform in Britain—the demand for an Act of Incorporation gathered strength. And it was Howe—now a provincial cabinet minister—who achieved this in 1841. Howe's successful defence of the libel suit reached beyond the freedom of the press, and helped convince him to become a politician, a calling that led to another great democratic milestone being achieved in Nova Scotia—responsible government.

Joseph Howe, Politician

The 1830s witnessed continuing and growing discontent with the Council of Twelve and led Howe into politics. In June 1836, Howe and William Annand were nominated by the freeholders of Middle Musquodoboit as candidates of the Reform Party—later known as

The Honourable Joseph Howe, journalist, politician, premier, and lieutenant-governor

Liberals—for Halifax County. In November, the assembly was dissolved and an election followed the next month. As was usual at the time, the election lasted two weeks, during which the candidates were permitted to address the electors on a daily basis.

During one of his many speeches on the stump, Howe outlined why he had entered politics. With regard to Halifax, he wanted "a system of responsible government—such an administration of our municipal affairs as will give to the lower and middle classes that influence in society to which they are entitled, and place all the officers who collect and expend the people's money under the people's control." For his province, he desired "those free institutions which, while they truly reflect the feelings of the people, shall best promote the happiness and prosperity of the country."

Howe noted that the great cornerstone of the British Constitution was "responsibility to the people. In England, one vote of the people's representatives turns out a ministry and a new one comes in, which is compelled to shape its policy by the views and wishes of the major-

Simon d'Entremont, one of the first two Acadian members of the House of Assembly, 1880

ity." In Nova Scotia, on the other hand, "we may record five hundred votes against our ministry and yet they sit unmoved, reproducing themselves from their own friends and connections and from a narrow party in the country, who, though opposed to the people, have a monopoly of influence and patronage."

Howe and Annand were both elected. For the first time, forerunners of true political parties appeared in a Nova Scotia election, with the governing Tories facing the Reformers, almost the single-handed creation of Howe. Among other Reformers taking their seats with Howe and Annand were the first two Acadians elected to the assembly, Simon d'Entremont and Frederick Robicheau. The earlier lifting of the final restrictions against Roman Catholics running for office in 1830 had opened the way for Acadians to enter the democratic process.

Howe took his seat in the House of Assembly on January 31, 1837. At the time, the executive council sat behind closed doors throughout the session, a practice that had been criticized for years to no avail. Howe seconded a motion to stop this practice, which the motion noted was "not only at variance with that of the House of Lords in England and that of several of the legislative councils in the other British North American colonies, but contrary to the spirit of the

British Constitution, and injurious to the interests and liberties of this country." The motion even offered to cover any expenses incurred for the accommodation of the public in the council chamber.

The resolution passed unanimously and was sent to the council. A few days later, the council replied. It denied the assembly the right to comment on its procedures, and maintained that whether the deliberations were open or closed was the concern only of the council and no one else. This set the tone for a debate that was to consume the energies of members of both Houses for several years. The council's reply spurred Howe to move his famous Twelve Resolutions, which brilliantly summed up the abuses under the current system of government and explained the need for reform, in a speech that lasted an hour and a half. The resolutions surprised the council, but were well-received throughout the province.

Debating Democracy

An animated debate followed on Howe's Twelve Resolutions. Virtually every member spoke, and the split was clearly along party lines. The Tories, led by James Boyle Uniacke and other accomplished speakers, attacked Howe. But Howe stood up to them, and held his own against much more experienced debaters. The resolutions passed, with minor

→

difficulties thrown in the way of a just and liberal system of education; and to the recent abortive attempts to abolish the illegal and unnecessary fees taken by judges of the supreme court.

4. *Resolved,* That while the population of this Province is composed...of [28,659] members of the Episcopal church, and [115,195] Dissenters...the appointments to the Council are always studiously arranged so as to secure to the members of the Church, embracing but one-fifth of the population, a clear and decided majority at the board. That there are now in that body eight members representing the Church; that the Presbyterians... have but three; the Catholics...have but one; while the Baptists...and the Methodists...and all the other sects and denominations, are entirely underrepresented, and shut out from influence in a body whose duty it is to legislate for all.

5. *Resolved,* That while the Catholic Bishop has no seat at the Council board, and while clergymen of all other denominations are, as they ought to be, carefully excluded, the Bishop of the Episcopal Church always has been, and still is a member.

amendments, and Howe moved for a committee to put them into the form of an address to the Crown.

While this was being done, a message arrived from the council that caused alarm in the assembly. It asked the House to rescind one of the resolutions, which referred to the council's "disposition to protect their own interests and emoluments at the expense of the public" and which members of council considered inconsistent with the rules of decorum. They warned that failure to do so would bring the business of government to a halt by the council's refusal to pass the revenue bills.

Everyone wondered how Howe would get out of the dilemma. If the assembly persisted, the revenue laws would expire and, without the authority to collect it, the revenue would be lost. If the assembly bowed to the wishes of the council, it would forfeit the right to convey to the Crown criticisms of the council whenever the council took offence. Howe's response was masterly.

He did not move to rescind the single offending resolution, but all twelve. Once they were withdrawn and the revenue bills passed, Howe asked for a committee to prepare an address to the Crown about the state of Nova Scotia. The resolutions had already served their purpose: they tested the opinions of the assembly, they went across the province—

along with the details of the debates they engendered—and they would go to England. The fact that they had been rescinded would make the assembly's case about the power of the council even stronger and point out the flaws in the colony's government.

Consequently, an address was composed to the king (containing the essentials of all twelve resolutions), passed, and sent to England on April 30. The council prepared a detailed defence of their actions to accompany the address, along with a strong statement of support for the council from Lieutenant-Governor Sir Colin Campbell.

The Rebellions of 1837

While the reformers in Nova Scotia pursued their goals by legitimate means, in Lower and Upper Canada radical reformers were taking drastic measures to realize their aims by following a completely different path from the British one. Frustrated with the lack of progress, militants took matters into their own hands.

In 1837, revolts against British rule occurred in Lower and Upper Canada after many years of political unrest and tension. Louis-Joseph Papineau led the rebellion in Lower Canada, while William Lyon Mackenzie was the leader in Upper Canada. These men and their followers favoured reform of the system that gave British governors

6. *Resolved,* That while the Dissenters…justly complain of a state of things so exclusive and insulting, they would regard its continuance with more indifference, if it did not lead to a general and injurious system of favouritism and monopoly.

7. *Resolved,* That two family connections embrace five members of the Council; that…five others were copartners in one mercantile concern; and to this circumstance may be attributed the failure of this Assembly to fix a standard of value, and establish a sound currency in the Province.

8. *Resolved,* That the Assembly of this Province have for years asserted…their right to control and distribute the casual and territorial revenues of the country.

9. *Resolved,* That…the presence of the Chief-Justice at the Council board is unwise and injurious, having a tendency to lessen the respect which the people ought to feel for the courts over which he presides.

10. *Resolved,* That the evils arising from the structure of His Majesty's Council, and the disposition evinced by some of its members

→

Joseph-Louis Papineau, the leader of the 1837 rebellion in Lower Canada, addressing a crowd

to protect their own interests and emoluments at the expense of the public, are heightened and rendered more injurious by the unconstitutional and insulting practice...of shutting out the people from their deliberations.

11. *Resolved,* That while the House has a true reverence for British institutions, and a desire to preserve to themselves and their children the advantages of that Constitution...they cannot but feel that those they represent participate but slightly in these blessings. But sad experience has taught them that, in this colony, the people and their representatives are powerless...and possessing no effectual control.

12. *Resolved,* That, as a remedy for these grievances, His Majesty be implored to take such steps, either by granting an elective Legislative Council, or by such other reconstruction of the local government as will ensure responsibility to the Commons, and confer upon the people of this Province, what they value above all other possessions, the blessings of the British Constitution.

and their colonial allies virtually complete power.

British troops quickly put down the rebellion in Lower Canada. Papineau and some of his leaders fled to the northern United States, and hundreds of his followers were rounded up. From his self-imposed exile, Papineau launched a second rebellion. The rebels attempted several incursions across the border, but due to poor organization and inadequate supplies, all were defeated.

The rebellion then spread to Upper Canada, where events were far less dramatic and violent than those in Lower Canada, essentially being put down by militia and volunteers. Like Papineau, Mackenzie also fled across the border. With the support of sympathetic Americans, Mackenzie and his rebels continued to conduct raids into Upper Canada for another year. Papineau and Mackenzie later returned to Canada, but many of their followers were hanged or deported to

Australia. After the rebellions had run their course, it was moderate reformers rather than radicals who ended up playing the biggest role in reconstructing the reform movement, in particular Louis-Hippolyte Lafontaine in Lower Canada and Robert Baldwin in Upper Canada.

Howe and the Rebellions of 1837

In 1835, two years before the rebellions in Lower and Upper Canada broke out, H. S. Chapman, one of the political agitators in Lower Canada, corresponded with Howe in an attempt to elicit from him a strong statement of the grievances of Nova Scotia's reformers. Howe suspected that the disgruntled Canadians did not simply have reform as their goal, but armed rebellion, leading to independence from Britain or annexation to the United States. His reply affirmed his belief that any severance should be the result of rational discourse. "We would rather," he wrote, "if the separation comes, that it should be the result of an amicable agreement, founded on an enlightened view of the circumstances by which all parties must content to be controlled."

Howe also emphasized his and his

William Lyon Mackenzie, the leader of the 1837 rebellion in Upper Canada

Louis-Hippolyte Lafontaine, a Reform leader in Lower Canada

Robert Baldwin, a Reform leader in Upper Canada

British troops under Colonel Wetherall advance to capture the rebel stronghold of St. Charles, November 25, 1837

A successful attack on the rebels at Dickinson Landing, Upper Canada, 1838

fellow colonials' attachment to Britain and loyalty to the Crown. "The people of Nova Scotia and New Brunswick," he noted, "are sincerely attached to the mother country, and disposed to cultivate towards her inhabitants the most friendly feelings." Howe had little time for the radical reformers in the Province of Canada, believing their actions were "absurd and ridiculous as well as mischievous." Howe chose the higher path—one of reason and perseverance—in his attempts to achieve responsible government for his home province.

When Howe's loyalty was questioned at the height of the rebellions, he published his letter to Chapman of two years earlier, effectively quashing those who equated reform with treason and rebellion. His display of support for the Crown and his warning of the failure of any armed insurrection resulted in the king's "cheerful assent" to most of the twelve measures proposed in the assembly's earlier address to the sovereign. The British despatches bearing this news arrived in Halifax in August 1837, but Lieutenant-Governor Sir Colin Campbell did not show them to Howe. Instead, he began talks with Howe about potential members of any new executive and legislative councils, should the king direct their creation. Campbell also indicated that he had been informed that there were insufficient men available to form two separate councils for the discharge of the executive and legislative functions.

If approved, the new legislative council would act as the upper house of the assembly, similar today to the Canadian Senate or the British House of Lords. Its members would be appointed, rather than elected, and would have to review and approve all legislation before it became law, as the assembly would also continue to do. The executive council, or Council of Twelve, would continue to operate much as it had before, its members acting as

A view of Halifax from the Mi'kmaq encampment at Tuft's Cove

close advisors to the governor and functioning similar to a cabinet. Some of its members were also the heads of government departments, such as the chief justice, treasurer, surveyor general, and collector of customs.

Change Begins

Howe quickly destroyed the lieutenant-governor's contention by drawing up proposed lists for each council. All members of the old executive council were on the new lists, as well as the leading men from all the important sectors of the province and various general interests that had been previously excluded. Howe showed conclusively that the formation of two separate councils was possible. In the end, Campbell forwarded a list of his own making, completely disregarding the earlier guidance of Colonial Secretary Lord Glenelg.

Briefly, Glenelg's directions were to avoid even the appearance of favouritism towards the Church of England in appointing councillors, to exclude all judges from the executive council, and to appoint not more than one member of any business to that council. When the names of the new councillors were published in the *Nova Scotia Gazette*, it became obvious that both the king's intentions and the

The Honourable Herbert Huntington, a leading Reformer

colonial secretary's instructions had been wilfully ignored.

When the session of 1838 opened in January, a twelve-man executive council was still in place, but a new nineteen-man appointed legislative council had been established by Campbell on orders from Britain. Both councils were filled with men supportive of the old ways of conducting government business, men who did not feel bound in any way to acknowledge the popular expressions of the people's will—this despite the fact that the executive council contained four men who were also members of the assembly. Only one member of the executive council from the assembly, Herbert Huntington, represented the majority in the assembly—the Reformers. In a break with tradition, the new legislative council now met in open session and not behind closed doors, and its debates were published in newspapers for the first time.

In March, the assembly debated a government resolution proposing that the province make permanent provision for members of the Civil List, a document that detailed certain senior government officials—such as the lieutenant-governor, provincial secretary, and judiciary—and their salaries. Previously, these officials had been paid from an annual parliamentary grant from Britain, which meant they were not subject to the assembly's control. In exchange for Nova Scotia agreeing to maintain and pay for these positions, the Crown would surrender to the province the last remaining monies it collected in the colony, known as the casual and territorial revenues.

During the debate, Howe pointed out his reservations to it, as he had on earlier occasions when the issue was discussed. He felt that the salaries—totalling £8,000—were too extravagant for a poor province, especially one that was £120,000 in debt. In newspaper articles published a few years earlier, he had pointed out that the pay scales established by the Colonial Office gave Nova Scotia's provincial secretary almost £2,000 and its chief justice £1,500 a year, while the wealthier American state of New York paid its corresponding officials only £375 and £500. In fact, Nova Scotia paid its chief justice more than the chief justice of the United States, and its provincial secretary more than any American official except the president.

Like Howe, Huntington also opposed the Civil List Bill and proposed an amendment in lieu—which subsequently passed in the assembly. Yet, despite the assembly's support, the legislative councillors did not feel they had any obligation to advise the lieutenant-governor to accept the assembly's bill. They maintained that their responsibility was simply to pass along the assembly's wishes.

Shortly afterwards, in May, Lord Durham was appointed as governor general of British North America, with a remit to recommend changes to the colonial governments as a result of the Lower and Upper Canada rebellions. His instructions detailed the composition of the new councils in the various colonies. They also showed the uncoordinated efforts of the Colonial Office, as they did not refer to or mention in any way the instructions given earlier to Sir Colin Campbell, which detailed councils of a different size. The directions to Durham stated that executive councils were to have nine members and the legislative ones fifteen—both less than the twelve- and nineteen-man councils already operating in Nova Scotia.

In accordance with this direction, the two Nova Scotia councils were immediately dissolved and new ones appointed by proclamation, containing the approved number of councillors. Huntington—the lone Reformer on the executive council—was one of those dropped; no doubt for his action on the government's proposed Civil List Bill. In addition, the new legislative council not only contained men who opposed the idea of responsible government but also the policy of the majority in the assembly.

The impasse between the assembly and the legislative council resulted in yet another address to the sovereign, the new queen—Victoria. In it, the assembly pointed out that, contrary to the wishes of the late king—her uncle—as expressed in official despatches to the lieutenant-governor, nothing had really changed in the way Nova Scotia was governed, with the exception of having two distinct bodies to discharge the legislative and executive functions. Members of the Church of England comprised one fifth of the population of the colony but had been in the overwhelming majority in the old council, and the new councils were not much of an improvement: five of nine executive council members and eight of fifteen on the legislative council—including the bishop—were Anglicans. Yet Lord Glenelg had clearly stated that "even the semblance of undue favour to any particular Church was to be avoided."

The direction to include "all the great interests of the Province; and the appointment of persons connected not merely with the capital, but with the other principal towns, and with the rural districts" had not been followed either. More than half the legislative council came from Halifax, six of its fifteen members were lawyers, and only two came from the agricultural sector.

Additionally, many members of the council were "known to be unfavourable to many of those reforms which the people of this Province anxiously desire in their institutions." Most of the address was taken up with financial matters, especially the salaries proposed for the Civil List. Members of the assembly regarded these amounts as a wasteful extravagance, one that continued the previous tradition of appointed office-holders bleeding the province dry financially. True reform had still not been achieved.

Chapter 10
The Growth of Reform

Lord Durham and his Famous Report

LORD DURHAM DIDN'T LAST LONG AS GOVERNOR general. He was sworn in on May 28, 1838, and resigned on November 30. During his brief time in office, delegates from the different North American colonies conferred with him, including four from Nova Scotia. In Nova Scotia, nothing had really changed and the session of January 1839 opened with the same councillors in power. In frustration, the Reformers in Nova Scotia decided to send a delegation to England to make their case in person, since it was now obvious that resolutions and addresses from the assembly accomplished nothing in the struggle for reasonable reform.

Joseph Howe, as leader of the Reformers, was the natural choice to head the delegation, but he decided not to go. He believed it was more important for him to remain in Nova Scotia to defend the delegation against the charges that would inevitably follow from the council. The assembly and the legislative council each sent two of their members to defend their interests. Herbert Huntington and William Young represented the assembly, while Alexander Stewart and Lewis Wilkins acted for the council.

The delegates sailed in the spring of 1839 to press their respective cases with the Colonial Office. They had to pay their own way, as the legislative council had rejected a request for a grant

1839
Durham Report presented; Howe writes series of letters to Lord Russell

1840
Reformers force Britain to recall Lieutenant-Governor Campbell, Lord Falkland replaces him

1841
Howe is elected speaker

LORD DURHAM

John George Lambton, first Earl of Durham, was a Liberal politician of independent means. His well-connected family lived off the income from several coal mines on their land in northeast England. Although of frail health as a boy, he joined the army before becoming a Member of Parliament in 1813. He remained an MP until 1828, when he was given the title Baron Durham.

Although now a member of the nobility, Durham was a political radical, dubbed "Radical Jack" by his colleagues. He supported the rise of the middle class, reform of the House of Commons, free trade, the rights of Catholics, and universal education. He served as Lord Privy Seal in the government of his father-in-law, Lord Grey, and helped draft the Reform Bill of 1832. He was ambassador to Russia for two years (1835–37) before being sent to the Province of Canada as governor general with a remit to investigate the rebellions of 1837 as Lord High Commissioner.

Lord Durham, governor general and author of the famous Durham Report

to offset the delegates' expenses, in retaliation for the assembly's refusal to pay for the council's counter-delegation. Neither side was prepared to give an inch. When Huntington and Young returned without any substantive changes to the composition of the legislative and executive councils, the Reformers were at a loss over their next step.

While the assembly and councils continued to disagree in Nova Scotia, changes were taking place elsewhere. In England, Lord Glenelg resigned as colonial secretary and was replaced by Lord Normanby. At the same time, Lord Durham's report was tabled in Parliament. It gratified Howe and the other reformers to learn that the system of responsible government they had been espousing for some time was strongly recommended by Durham. Those opposed to Durham's idea of responsible government—the House of Lords, Tories, jealous rivals, officials in the colonies—attacked his proposals.

Durham's "Report on the Affairs of British North America" contained three main recommendations: to unite Lower and Upper Canada with one legislature (a long-standing desire of British Canadians, especially the mercantile class), to anglicize the French minority, and to grant responsible government to the colonies. Although he had expected to find a "contest between a government and a people," Durham instead "found a struggle, not of principles, but of races." He believed that before changing any laws or institutions, it was first necessary to end "the deadly animosity that now separates the inhabitants of Lower Canada into hostile divisions of French and English."

Once the two colonies were united, he argued, their powers could be significantly increased and ruled by responsible government. Responsible government would consist of the governor general as a figurehead, a legislative assembly elected by the people with the majority holding power, and a cabinet made up of elected representatives—in effect, the form of government found in Canada today.

Initially, British authorities refused to grant responsible government to their North American colonies, although they did agree to unite Lower and Upper Canada. The Act of Union was passed in 1840 and the Province of Canada was created the next year. Lord Durham's most far-reaching recommendation—the introduction of responsible government—was, unfortunately, still further down the road.

Howe and the Durham Report

Howe gave his opinion of the Durham Report in the pages of the *Novascotian* on April 11, 1839. He had read Durham's "admirable exposition of the state of the British colonies in North America with a higher estimate of the powers of the noble Lord and a more sanguine anticipation of the ultimate termination of colonial misrule than we have ever ventured to form." He believed no colonist could read the report—and he wished a copy was in the hands of every family head in Nova Scotia—without recognizing "the features of that system which has now become contemptible in the eyes of every man of common understanding, [and] who has no interest in keeping it up."

The report had a remedy for the state of conflict between the people and the local executives, "being perfectly *simple* and eminently *British*." It was, he wrote, "to let the *majority* and not the *minority* govern, and compel every Governor to select his advisers from those who *enjoy the confidence of the people* and can *command a majority in the popular branch*." For its part, the province's legislative council passed a series of resolutions condemning the report, as well as one disapproving of a union of the colonies.

By now, Lord John Russell, a great reformer, was the British home secretary. Russell's earlier efforts on behalf of the reformers had resulted in many Liberal seats in the 1830 elections in Britain. He was one of four members of government tasked to prepare the first Reform Bill in 1832, and was given the honour of proposing it in Parliament. In June 1839, Russell introduced measures to settle Canadian affairs. They recommended a union of the Canadas, but stopped short of allowing responsible government.

Reformers in Upper and Lower Canada were stunned and disappointed. They held Russell in great esteem for his earlier efforts on behalf of reform, and expected him to support the idea of responsible government for the North American colonies. Russell's refusal to grant responsible government—given in a speech he made on June 3—stemmed from his belief that the governor general could be put in an impossible situation, especially in matters of foreign affairs and international trade, if the assembly pressed for action contrary to his instructions from the sovereign.

Howe and His Letters to Lord Russell

Howe viewed the situation somewhat differently from his colleagues. As far as he was concerned, Russell simply did not understand the question, the result of having studied it only from an imperial, rather than a colonial, point of view. Howe was sure that if Russell and the other leading minds in Britain truly understood the issue, they would not want to maintain the method of administration that generated oppression and discontent in the five North American colonies.

With his characteristic energy, Howe immediately set about to inform Russell and his colleagues of the error of their ways. He sent four lengthy letters to Russell dated September 18, 1839, which were quickly published in colonial newspapers. In them, he expertly refuted all of Russell's objections to responsible government in the colonies one by one. He then printed the letters as pamphlets, and sent them to all members of the Commons and the Lords, as well as to newspapers, clubs, and reading rooms throughout Britain.

As a result of agitation from Lower and Upper Canada, Lord Russell's despatches of October 1839 implied the conferment of new constitutions on all the colonies. In the united Canadas, the governor general advised Parliament that the queen had declared that colonial government was to be administered "in accordance with the well-understood wishes and interests of the people." In New Brunswick, Lieutenant-Governor Sir John Harvey immediately informed the heads of government departments that their appointments would, in future, be held based on public confidence. In Nova Scotia, nothing happened, and the executive council went about its business as if nothing had changed.

Howe Challenges the Lieutenant-Governor

In February 1840, Howe moved four resolutions in the assembly regarding the remodelling of the executive council, which ended with the statement that "the Executive Council, as at present constituted, does not enjoy the confidence of the Commons [assembly]." James Boyle Uniacke, a leading Tory, agreed with Howe and said he was willing to "try the experiment." A lengthy debate followed, in which all members agreed that the existing system of government was indefensible and Russell's despatches did confer new constitutions on the colonies. The motion passed by a vote of thirty to twelve, although some who agreed with the justice of it voted against it or abstained.

Lieutenant-Governor Campbell's reply to the approved resolution was astonishing. "Having no reason to believe," he declared, "that any alteration has taken place in the sentiments of Her Majesty's Government in this respect, I do not feel myself at liberty to adopt any other course than to refer you to the despatch already alluded to as containing their decision. Justice, however, to the Executive Council, leads me to say that I have had every reason to be satisfied with the advice and assistance which they have at all times afforded me."

Campbell's obstinacy in establishing responsible government in Nova Scotia echoed the views of Governor Charles Lawrence

Lieutenant-Governor Sir Colin Campbell, who was forced from office by the efforts of the Reformers

and his attempts to delay the establishment of representative government over eighty years earlier.

As a result, Uniacke, the government leader in the House and a member of the executive council, immediately resigned his seat on the council. His place as the leading Tory spokesman was taken by James W. Johnston, who had generally been viewed as a moderate Conservative. In the House, Howe rose and declared that from that hour on they could date the establishment of the very principles for which they had been fighting, and that no member of the assembly could continue in future to hold a seat on the council against the wishes of the House. He also gave notice that he would move an address directly to the governor general, but quickly thought the better of it and recommended one last address to Campbell before adopting a course that would inevitably bring censure upon Campbell and result in his removal.

The address, which passed by twenty-nine to ten after some debate, emphasized that

care of the Queen's prerogative, the conservation of treaties, the military defence, and the execution of the imperial Acts; the local administration being left in the hands of those who understood it and who were responsible...

...the Cabinet in a colony [i.e., the executive council] is an *official* party who have the power for ever to keep themselves and their friends in office and to keep all others out, even though nineteen out of every twenty of the population are against them...

...for this body I propose to substitute one sustained by at least a majority of the electors; whose general principles are known and approved; whom the Governor may dismiss, whenever they exceed their powers; and who may be discharged by the people whenever they abuse them; who, instead of laying the blame, when attacked, upon the Governor, or the Secretary of State, shall be bound, as in England, to stand up and defend, against all comers, every appointment made and every act done under their administration...

The magnificent Red Chamber in Province House, which was the meeting place of the legislative council

The House of Assembly in Province House, where Nova Scotia's elected representatives have met since 1819

Russell's despatches not only gave Campbell "the power to remodel the Executive Council, but make such changes as are required, to ensure harmony between the executive and legislative branches of the government, imperative." It also accused Campbell of using a despatch sent the previous August by Russell's predecessor as colonial secretary as an excuse for not making changes—changes that had already occurred in the Province of Canada and New Brunswick.

The gravity of the situation still failed to register with the lieutenant-governor. "By adopting the course you suggest," he replied, "I should practically recognize a fundamental change in the colonial constitution, which I cannot certainly discover to have been designed by the despatch of [Lord Russell in October], in the manner and to the extent supposed by you." Campbell did not feel he had the authority to make such sweeping changes as the assembly suggested, but did promise to send the assembly's addresses and resolutions to the British government.

Sir Colin Campbell's continued intransigence thoroughly frustrated and exhausted Howe and his fellow Reformers. They agreed to move an address requesting the sovereign to remove the lieutenant-governor. If the other members of the executive council had followed Uniacke's example and resigned, a new council would have had to be designated. The power of the assembly would have been asserted and responsible government would have come into effect in 1840, rather than several years later. But the other members of the council were quite prepared to see Campbell sacrificed rather than have him surrounded by advisors who commanded a majority in the assembly.

In March, Uniacke sent a letter to his constituents explaining why he had resigned from the executive council: "...as a member of the Assembly," he wrote, "I owed it to the House to come out of a body which had been politically

The Arrival of Governor General Lord Sydenham at the opening of the Union Parliament, Kingston, 1841

condemned by such an overwhelming majority." Howe supported and admired Uniacke's action, even though previously there had been many differences of opinion between them. The two became firm colleagues and worked together in future assemblies.

At the end of March, following a sharp debate, Howe moved an address to the Crown that was carried almost two to one in the assembly. The address contained the wording of four key documents: the resolutions forwarded to Campbell in February, his reply, the assembly's response to Campbell's reply, and the lieutenant-governor's final answer. In closing, it requested Queen Victoria to "repress these absurd attempts to govern Provinces by the aid and for the exclusive benefits of minorities" and asked her "to remove Sir Colin Campbell and send to Nova Scotia a Governor who will not only represent the Crown, but carry out its policy with firmness and good faith" as the only remedy "to establish harmony between the Executive and Legislature of this Province."

The Reformers had taken an extreme step, and one that was not to be without its consequences locally. Campbell was well liked and had many friends. Some moderates who had previously supported

Elections during the struggle for responsible government often developed into brawls

the Reformers now felt they had gone too far. Meetings were held across the province in an attempt to retain the lieutenant-governor. Howe addressed one of them at the Mason's Hall in Halifax, at which Solicitor General James Johnston defended Campbell and the council. It was the first of many contests that were to follow between the two.

At about this time, Howe was offered a seat on the executive council, providing he would renounce the "heretical" principles he had enunciated in his four letters to Lord Russell the previous September. He declined. In May, word was received that Lord Russell had decided not to present the assembly's address to the queen and that Campbell would remain. Then, a month later, rumours circulated that the lieutenant-governor would be returning to England. In early July, Governor General Charles Poulett Thompson—soon to be elevated to the peerage as Lord Sydenham—arrived in Halifax on his way to the Province of Canada, with direction from Lord Russell to resolve the issue.

Thompson sent for the leading men of both parties and asked for their opinions. Someone had given Howe's pamphlet containing his letters to Russell to Thompson, as proof of the absurdity of Howe's views. During his discussion with Thompson, Howe offered to read the pamphlet to him and asked him to object to any points with which he disagreed. Although Thompson intervened occasionally for further discussion or explanation, in the end there was nothing to which he objected. By the time Thompson left the province, it was obvious that Campbell would be recalled and that changes would take place.

A New Lieutenant-Governor

The new lieutenant-governor, Viscount Falkland, described as a "thorough Whig," arrived in September 1840. Four members of the executive council (Jeffery, Collins, Cogswell, Tobin) who did not hold seats in the assembly or legisla-

A miniature portrait of Lord Falkland

tive council were asked to resign so they could be replaced with men who enjoyed the support and confidence of the people. Howe was one of them. He agreed, subject to four conditions: that James McNab should also join, that the government should bring down a bill to incorporate Halifax, that other Reformers should join the executive council as vacancies became available, and that all council members should hold their seats as long as they had the confidence of the public, as shown by their party's standing in the assembly, rather than for life.

In an address to the people, Lord Falkland stated it was his intention to ensure Nova Scotians would enjoy the same "municipal rights and privileges" as the people of Britain. The assembly was dissolved and elections followed, a two-week process at the time. Opposition to the Reformers was still strong, especially from the supporters of Campbell and the four executive councillors who had been removed. The Reformers took the majority of seats (thirty to twenty) and Howe and three other Reformers became members of the executive council. When the new assembly convened for the first time on February 3, 1841, Howe was elected speaker by a slim majority of two over James Boyle Uniacke.

The Honourable James Johnston, Joseph Howe's key rival

It was a great victory for Howe, as a newcomer to politics, to be chosen over the heads of several more seasoned members. Both Howe and Uniacke sat on the executive council, although neither had any salaried offices in the government. Technically, as speaker, Howe should not have been a member of the council, as in Britain the speaker was not a member of the cabinet (although he was a member of the Privy Council). When this discrepancy was pointed out to Howe, he offered to resign from one of them "if the House by resolution should say that the offices were incompatible." The issue was debated, but withdrawn once it became clear that the majority did not want to lose his services in either appointment. It looked as if Nova Scotia was about to embark on a new era in the way it was governed.

The process started immediately. Assembly members on the council agreed that they would hold their seats only as long as they held the confidence of the public; they would prepare and submit measures to the legislature, accepting responsibility for their success or failure; the lieutenant-governor could avoid any unconstitutional pressure on him by demanding their resignation; and the House might compel them to resign at any time as well. Unfortunately, not all members of the council agreed with this interpretation.

In a debate in the Upper House, one councillor denied that the sort of responsibility that the assembly had asked for in its resolutions or that Howe had described in his pamphlet had been conceded. James Johnston made similar statements in his speech, and denied that any constitutional changes had taken place. "The three branches [assembly, legislative council, executive council] will continue as before," he solemnly declared, continuing, "the change simply is that it becomes the duty of the representatives of Her Majesty [lieutenant-governors] to ascertain the wishes and feelings of the people through their representatives and to make the measures of Government conform to these as far as is consistent with his duty to the mother country."

Alexander Stewart, another member of the government, agreed with him, and said, "No change had been made in the constitution of the country and the principles of responsibility had not been conceded. Responsible government, in a Colony, was responsible nonsense—it was independence." If the assembly voted non-confidence, he maintained, it would merely be "a matter of taste and feeling" for the executive council to determine whether it should resign, or for the lieutenant-governor to decide to dismiss it. Stewart also stated that the only kinds of responsibility in a colony were those of the governor to the colonial secretary and the executive council to the governor.

In response, Howe noted that, if the assembly followed its stated beliefs, every future government would be dependent upon the assembly to continue in office. "It is not a matter of taste or opinion," he replied, "when the House passed a vote of censure, whether the Council should resign or not." Although it might be a matter of taste for the governor to either dissolve the House or change his council, the councillors themselves would have "no taste or discretion in the matter," he declared. They were bound to submit their resignations, and if they did not, the governor would send for them "in half an hour."

Declarations like Stewart's caused great distrust in the assembly and throughout the province. Those who made them continued to misunderstand—wilfully or otherwise—the changes that had taken place. As speaker, Howe had his hands full. In February 1841, he reiterated and defined the principles on which the new administration had been formed and offered those councillors who opposed them a choice.

They could retire from the council, agree with his definition, or demand his retirement. In regard to the speeches made in the Upper House, Howe did not mince his words. "I care not what has been expressed by others in other places," he declared, "...but if any man in the colony, in this House or the other, says that there is no change in the constitution, the person so speaking does not state what is the fact."

To clarify matters, Howe spoke for two hours the next day and summarized recent events by noting that:

> A vote of this House, now, may place the Governor in this position: he shall discharge his Council, change his policy, or dissolve the House. That is the system which every man of the majority had in view, and it is truly British. Sir Colin Campbell would do neither of the three. He evaded the despatch by which the new policy was announced. His Council would not resign; he would not dismiss them; he shrank from dissolving the House; and finally, all parties in the colony shifted the responsibility off their own shoulders to those of the Secretary of State. That system is at an end. The responsibility now rests on the Governor and his Council, and whether it is called direct or indirect, it is sufficient to ensure good government.

Shortly afterwards, the first benefits of the new system were realized when a government bill to incorporate Halifax passed with a large majority in both Houses, overturning the defeat of a similar bill two years earlier. But all was not rosy. An attempt by Howe to introduce free schools into the province, supported by assessment, was soundly defeated. Such changes would have to wait.

This session of the legislature closed on April 10. Although the accepted wisdom is that responsible government did not occur in Nova Scotia until 1848—seven years later—some authorities maintain that this session was, in fact, the first under responsible government.

Chapter 11
The Struggle for Responsible Government

Ebb & Flow

By now, both Whigs and Tories in Britain had accepted the idea of the gradual introduction of some form of responsible government as the solution to the grievances of the colonists, and were not prepared to go back to the old system. In Nova Scotia, the struggle for responsible government was gaining ground daily, and the session of 1842 opened with high hopes for harmony. At this stage, a coalition was essentially running the province, as both Tories and Reformers served on the executive council. Although Lord Falkland had stated his preference for this type of government, the main question was whether men with strong opposing views, who sat on the same body, could cooperate to allow the government to function effectively.

A test of the new system occurred when a bankruptcy law bill introduced by the government passed in the legislative coun-

Halifax, circa 1840

Joseph Howe at an open air meeting

cil, but was defeated in the assembly. Opponents of the government asked if council members intended to resign, and notices were put forward of hostile resolutions to test the strength of the administration. Although these were withdrawn, supporters of the government thought it was best to ascertain the strength of the administration and moved a vote of confidence, hoping to break up any unfriendly groupings in the process. A full debate followed in which the government was sustained.

Meanwhile, some members of the legislative council continued to attempt to water down the principles of responsible government by declaring themselves not responsible to the assembly. Howe threatened to resign as speaker and put the system to the test by allowing the majority in the assembly to force the councillors to resign, an act that would result in the overturn of the government. The reactionaries backed off, and one of the councillors, E. M. Dodd, read out a statement in council that reaffirmed the authority of the assembly.

Dodd stated that if, after full deliberation on a matter that involved responsibility, the assembly declared it had no confidence in the executive council through a vote, either a change of government or dissolution of the assembly would occur. If, after an election, the assembly had the same point of view, the lieutenant-governor would have to appoint new councillors who met with the assembly's—and, by extension, the province's—approval, to carry out the work of government. Dodd's statement, humorously known as the "Doddean Confession of Faith," defused the situation— at least in the two Houses. Outside, it was a different matter.

Several of the former executive council members who had lost their positions in the new government when Lord Falkland brought Reformers into it resented the loss of status that accompanied their demotion. These were wealthy men with high social standing in the community, and they—along with relatives, friends, and supporters—continued to agitate against the perceived injustice to which they had been subjected, especially in the press. As well, the establishment's concern that holders of government appointments—including offices that had formerly been regarded as hereditary—might lose their positions under the new system added to their agitation.

Legislative Councillor E.M. Dodd, who defused a tense situation during the session of 1842 by reaffirming the authority of the assembly

In June 1842, a series of nine letters appeared in the *Novascotian* signed by "A Constitutionalist." In them, the writer successfully refuted every charge brought against the government by other newspapers' writers. He also belittled the desires of fathers who wanted to pass on their offices to their sons, despite the limited abilities of many of them. Although the authorship of these letters has never been acknowledged, they were widely assumed at the time—and still are—to be written by Howe.

That fall, Howe accepted the appointment of collector of colonial revenue, a move that resulted in his resignation as speaker when the assembly next met in January 1843. The Tories had been pressuring Falkland to keep the collectorship in the Binney family, as the incumbent was not expected to live long. It had been one of the appointments specifically mentioned in the Constitutionalist's let-

The Honourable Sir William Young, an ally of Joseph Howe's

ters, with the comment that Falkland was "a cool sort of person, not easily frightened when he knows he is right." Howe knew he was about to get the post—and the Tories likely guessed it—which made his taunts in the press all the more galling to them. To the Tories, the appointment of Howe and his Reform colleagues to government posts was clear indication that the movement for responsible government, which the Reformers claimed was based on lofty principles, was really nothing more than a fight for salaried offices for the Reformers.

When William Young, a member of the executive council, replaced Howe as speaker, a resolution was passed that decreed the speaker could no longer be a member of council. Young resigned immediately, setting a precedent that continues today. Shortly afterwards, the government introduced the Qualification Bill, intended to extend the privilege of running for the assembly to certain persons who had previously been denied it by right of not being property owners in the constituency in which they wished to stand.

Although Howe remained generally unenthusiastic during the session of 1843, he made a speech heartily endorsing the proposal, which he felt was fully in accordance with British principles and "an important part of the system which we have been endeavouring to establish." Several members voted against the bill because they felt it might give undue influence to wealthy men from Halifax who had the money to run for country seats, but it passed and became law by a narrow margin.

Howe versus Lord Falkland

As the first session of 1843 drew to a close, the Tories announced they would introduce a motion at the next session to exclude customs and excise officers from the assembly, a move that would have precluded Howe from sitting. To Howe, this was another example of the conflict between members of the coalition, who were supposed to be united for the betterment of the colony, yet continued to let petty party politics trump good government. Earlier in the session he had told Falkland that something more was "required to make a strong Administration than nine men, treating each other courteously at a round table—there is the assurance of good faith—towards each other—of common sentiments, and kindly feelings..." In response, Howe gave notice of an amendment that stated that the time had come for "the formation of a Provincial cabinet, united in sentiment, acting in harmony in both branches of the Legislature, and in a [way] calculated to obtain and secure the confidence of the people."

This portrait of James William Johnston hangs besides the Speaker's chair in the legislative assembly

Although Howe was merely reacting to the goading of the Tories, his motion thoroughly upset Falkland, who wondered why Howe had neither informed him nor Howe's colleagues beforehand of his amendment. Falkland viewed the public call for a cabinet as an attack on the coalition government that he favoured that would weaken the administration.

The lieutenant-governor was firmly against party government in "this comparatively petty province"—as he had insultingly termed Nova Scotia in a despatch to Britain—and warned both Tories and Reformers that he would consider anyone who made a move towards party government as having deserted him. In Howe's opinion, it was the Tories who had been against the idea of coalition government from the start, and took every opportunity to ensure its failure. Relations between Howe and Falkland were never the same again. James Johnston, leader of the Tories and attorney general in the coalition government, replaced Howe in Falkland's favour.

While Howe was making visits around the province that October, Falkland dissolved the assembly without consulting the Reformers. In his despatches to Colonial Secretary Lord Stanley, Falkland claimed it was the only way to avoid immediately forming a party government, which he said the Reformers were trying to force on him. His despatches presented Johnston as the hero and Howe the villain.

When Howe learned of the dissolution, he thought it an imprudent and fatal step on the part of the young peer to dissolve an assembly that had done no wrong, given no offence, and sustained the administration with overwhelming majorities. In the election that followed, the voters of Halifax County returned Howe without opposition. James Johnston, who had resigned from the legislative council to run for the assembly, was also elected, setting the stage for Howe–Johnston confrontations for the next twenty years.

In the election the Tories converted a minority of nine seats to a majority of one. In an attempt to force party government on the lieutenant-governor, Howe called on Lord Falkland after the election and offered to either resign or form a government, less those who strongly opposed him. Falkland wavered, and wanted to keep the same councillors as before the election. Howe agreed to Falkland's wishes, although the lieutenant-governor's subsequent actions made Howe's eventual decision easy for him.

Falkland then took a perverse course of action that flew in the face of the concept of the majority of councillors being from the party that held the majority in the assembly. He appointed Johnston's brother-in-law and fellow Tory, Mather Byles Almon—who was known to be opposed to party government—to seats on the executive and legislative councils on December 21. Why he did this has been subject to speculation. Perhaps he intended to demonstrate his control of the situation to his new Tory superiors in Britain and secure their approval and praise. Howe, McNab, and Uniacke immediately resigned from the council, the latter having irreversibly joined the Reformers. In the end, Falkland's headstrong actions ironically advanced the cause of party government over coalition government, a course of action he had been determined to avoid. By extension, his actions also hastened the advent of responsible government.

James Boyle Uniacke, who was the first premier of Nova Scotia under responsible government

While Howe defended Falkland's right to make any appointments to the council he chose, he felt that Almon's elevation marked a change in the policy of any new councillors being selected from the Reformers to increase their representation on the council, a policy that had already been approved in principle. Howe declared he could not continue to serve on the same council as Almon. He also offered to resign his appointment as collector of impost and duties for Halifax.

In the face of these resignations from the council, Falkland should have offered the vacancies to Johnston to fill, as the leader of the majority in the assembly, and then sought the vindication of the assembly for his actions. Instead, the impetuous young lord brought the matter to public attention through a letter in the newspapers, in which he justified his appointment of Almon. Within a very short time, relations between Falkland and the Reformers—especially Howe—had deteriorated beyond any hope of redemption.

Since Falkland had moved the issue into a more public arena, however, Howe felt obliged to reply. He pointed out that when he took his seat on the executive council, although his party held a "considerable" majority in the assembly, they had only two or three council members, while those who formed a minority in the House had six. Such inequality had caused great dissatisfaction among Reform Party members, but they continued to support the government based on the pledge made by British authorities that as vacancies occurred, the imbalance would be redressed.

Yet, after the latest election, when the Reformers held nearly half the seats in the assembly, they had only two seats on the council. Howe was prepared to accept this temporarily, but when a vacancy occurred and Almon was appointed, it was obvious that the stated policy had somehow changed and that "justice was not to be done."

As far as "party government" was concerned, Howe noted that for many years prior to Falkland's arrival, "party government existed here in its most offensive form; the minority having all the executive influence and the entire distribution of patronage, while the great body of the people had nothing but a representation of two to one in the Assembly."

Meanwhile, now that the Tories were returned to power in Britain, the Conservative press agitated for them to remove Falkland (a Whig), restore the old council, and turn out the Reformers. Such actions would have resulted in the legislature having no influence on the government.

Howe and his Liberal colleagues realized that they were on the verge of losing all they had fought for if the composition of the council bore no resemblance to the representation of both parties in the assembly, or if a change in the majority of the assembly did not result in a similar change in the council. They decided that they needed to state their case to the public. Although Howe had sold the *Novascotian* in 1841, leading Reformers induced him to resume its editorship as well as that of the *Morning Chronicle,* a recent publication. Howe agreed to use the two newspapers to defend the popular cause of responsible government and disseminate Liberal policies. Howe also attacked Lord Falkland, with the aim of defeating his supporters at the next election.

On May 20, 1844, Howe published a poem entitled "Lord of the Bed-Chamber" in the *Novascotian.* In it, Howe lampooned the perplexities and conflicting feelings experienced by the lieutenant-governor (the Lord of the Bed-Chamber) and his advisors during a two-week debate in the assembly. Tories at home and in Britain universally reacted in horror. Howe's criticism of Falkland was destined to become a classic of political literature. Unfortunately, it probably hurt his chances of becoming the first premier under responsible government by unfairly tarnishing him as intemperate and indiscreet.

Shortly afterwards, five of Howe's Liberal friends—Uniacke, McNab, Huntington, George Brennan, and Michael Tobin—were offered seats on the council, including the position of solicitor general, providing they left Howe out. Uniacke spoke for them all when he declined. The Reformers would take their chances on the hustings. Just as Howe had predicted, Falkland was in a mess of his own making. In order to avoid party government, he had ended up with an executive council made up only of Tories and he could find no one but more Tories to replace them.

In July, Howe moved a motion declaring that the council "as at present constituted does not enjoy the confidence of this Assembly." Before a vote could be called, Falkland prorogued the session and visited the countryside, hoping to drum up support for his government's waning fortunes. Everywhere he met with a lack of the enthusiasm that normally greeted a visit from the vice-regal representative. Meanwhile, a parliamentary debate had occurred in the British House of Commons in June that helped the cause of Howe and his colleagues—the government reiterated its support for responsible government in the Province of Canada. Before the year was out, most political observers in Nova Scotia believed that Falkland would either have to leave the province or take Reformers back onto the council.

When the 1845 session of the legislature opened on February 1, a despatch that Lord Falkland had sent to the colonial secretary in August was laid before the House. In it, Falkland had unfairly and incorrectly stigmatized Howe, and suggested that the leading Reformers would enter the council even if it did not include Howe. Howe was outraged and the letter led to a stormy session. In a speech in the assembly he decried the young lord's actions, stating that the course Falkland took would "never be imitated by any colonial governor, certainly not by any wise one."

Thirteen days of turbulent debate followed, which descended to a personal level based on the unprecedented release of the contents of Falkland's despatch. In return, Howe was ruthless in his assault on the government and the lieutenant-governor, now that they had lowered the tone of the debate by their unrelenting attacks on his character.

The close results on a resolution following the debate clearly contradicted Falkland's contention to Colonial Secretary Lord Stanley that the opposition was growing weak, as well as the claim that the Reformers were prepared to sacrifice Howe. It was, in fact, the government that was growing weak, especially in the countryside. At election time, three of Falkland's supporters lost, to be replaced by three of Howe's friends.

The long-established and well-attended colonial tradition of the lieutenant-governor's New Year's Day levee was dispensed with in 1846 over fears that few would turn up, a clear sign of the low opinion the people held of Lord Falkland. The new session of the legislature opened on January 10 and Falkland attempted to appoint a new treasurer for life, in defiance of Lord Russell's direction that the position should be held only for the life of a Parliament. Another sharp debate followed between the Conservatives and the Reformers, with Howe displaying his usual eloquence.

Howe's jabs at Lord Falkland became more barbed when he noted that "the strong minds that nature produces generally stay at home, while the weaker ones, that can be spared in England, the gleanings of the peerage or the army, are often sent to govern and must succumb to a range of intellect beyond the elevation

Lieutenant-Governor Sir John Harvey, who replaced Viscount Falkland

of their own," and "without undervaluing the rulers who may be sent, I may safely prophesy that they will generally find here more intellect and information than they bring."

Falkland's troubled days were coming to an end. He dispensed with the usual levee on the Queen's Birthday and departed at his own request on August 1 for a post in India. His successor was Sir John Harvey, an old soldier and former lieutenant-governor of Prince Edward Island, New Brunswick, and Newfoundland, where he had shown tact and good sense. The actions of Howe and his colleagues had forced the queen's representative to resign. Could responsible government be far behind?

The Reformers Come to Power

In the fall of 1846, Lieutenant-Governor Harvey suggested a coalition government, similar to the ones he had worked with successfully in New Brunswick and Newfoundland. The Reformers rebuffed his offer, confident that the upcoming elections would be in their favour. Shortly afterwards, Howe sent two more letters to Lord Russell, which were published in the leading newspapers of British North America. In them, Howe asked for "a rigid enforcement of British practice, by the imperial authorities, on every governor," who should be "free to select their advisers from any of the parties which exist." He then cautioned, "let it be understood that they must hold the balance even; that they must not become partisans themselves."

While Howe's letters were on their way to Britain, a November despatch from Colonial Secretary Earl Grey was on its way to Harvey. Although the Reformers were not to know its specific contents for several months, it was just what they had desired for so long: a clear, unequivocal, written agreement to their demands for responsible government. In it the British at long last admitted that self-government was inevitable, noting that it was "neither possible nor desirable to carry on the Government of any of the British Provinces in North America in opposition to the opinions of the inhabitants." Although the last obstacle to responsible government had finally been removed, the Reformers were not aware of it for some time.

Despite this direction, Harvey persisted in his efforts to form a coalition government. He asked his executive council members to assist him in the formation of a "mixed Government, including the talented and influential of all parties" and to propose to him the names they would recommend to fill existing vacancies, and claimed that a fair distribution would constitute the basis of the proposed coalition.

The governing Tories did nothing with this suggestion, other than to offer up the solicitor general's office, as the incumbent—Mather Byles Almon, the cause of the controversy in 1844 when he was appointed—was prepared to retire. At the same time, the council members argued for life tenure for themselves. This was hardly a fair distribution; the Reformers had nearly half the House.

During the session Johnston introduced the Simultaneous Polling

Bill, designed so that everyone voted at the same time. It was passed, significantly improving the way elections were run. The session closed near the end of March in preparation for the upcoming August elections. Howe threw himself into the effort in his typical enthusiastic fashion, campaigning not only in his own riding but elsewhere in the province in support of his colleagues.

The Tories, mindful that the old order was on the verge of destruction, also threw everything into the fight. Liquor flowed freely across the province, a boat sailed along the eastern shore distributing goods to secure votes, and the blacks at Hammonds Plains—who were ignored most of the time—received special attention from the Tories. But in the end, the Reformers' hard work paid off, and they were returned with a majority, winning twenty-nine of fifty-one seats.

The ministers who lost the election tried to maintain their status as the government and clung to power as long as they could instead of retiring gracefully, even petitioning the colonial secretary in Britain with their objections. In fact, following tradition they remained in office until the next session of the general assembly.

When the new House met in January 1848, William Young was elected speaker over the objections of Attorney General Johnston, who claimed that Young was too partisan. A couple of days after the Throne Speech, John Uniacke moved an amendment to it that stated the present executive council did not enjoy the confidence of the people. A debate followed, after which a historic vote was taken. By a majority of twenty-eight to twenty-one, the first successful vote of confidence in British North America was passed on February 2, a vote that turned out the administration and replaced it with the opposition. The old executive council resigned and Uniacke was asked to form a new one. With Uniacke as attorney general, the council—announced on February 2—included Joseph Howe as provincial secretary, James McNab, Herbert Huntington, Michael Tobin, Hugh Bell, William DesBarres, Lawrence Doyle, and George Young.

For the first time in their history, the Reformers (who now usually referred to themselves as Liberals) surrounded the lieutenant-governor and had free access to the Colonial Office. True responsible government had finally arrived in Nova Scotia. The right of any party commanding a parliamentary majority to form a cabinet and administer the affairs of the province was confirmed. Howe noted that this had been achieved with "not a pane of glass broken," ignoring the role the Rebellions of 1837—where much more than glass had been shattered—had played in the overall process. Responsible government followed in the Province of Canada on March 11, a month after Nova Scotia. Prince Edward Island achieved it in 1851, New Brunswick in 1854, and Newfoundland in 1855.

Yet what had occurred by a peaceful—though prolonged—revolution in Nova Scotia and Canada was still fervently wished for in many countries of continental Europe. In the summer of 1848 a number of revolutionary movements that had been simmering beneath the surface boiled over into open revolt against many of the crowned heads of Europe. The revolutions began in France, and then spread to Germany, Italy, and the Austrian Empire. They all ended in failure, followed by severe repressive measures. At the same time as liberals in Nova Scotia rejoiced over their progress, liberals in Europe became disillusioned and their cause was set back.

Chapter 12
Responsible Government and Beyond

Adapting to Responsible Government

THE LIBERALS DID NOT VIEW THE ATTAINMENT of responsible government in Nova Scotia as the end of their quest. Howe announced his hope that the province would become a "Normal School" (the name for a teacher's college at the time) for the rest of the colonies. The Conservatives were not ready to relinquish control without a fight, and threw up numerous roadblocks in the transition of political institutions to responsible government. But the Liberals gradually overcame opposition, and succeeded in getting their chief measure—the departmental bills—passed in February 1849.

The reorganization of the various government departments had long been a goal of the Liberals and was the very cornerstone of the new system of responsible government. Their intention was to establish the means by which adequate control by the majority over the departments that actually ran the affairs of the province would be assured. This would be accomplished by having sufficient public officers on the executive council. Simply put, the system they wanted was government by heads of departments—not unlike the way Nova Scotia is governed today.

The Tories vehemently opposed this reorganization, as they maintained that departmental heads who were members of both the assembly and the council would have an undue influence in those bodies, and could block any scrutiny into their conduct. The

Dr. Charles Tupper, who opposed Howe's views of confederation

Liberals scoffed at the idea that officials whose conduct was constantly under the examination of their opponents in the assembly, and whose resignation automatically followed an unfavourable vote in that body, could possibly evade accountability for any inappropriate actions. The Liberals' view won the day, and the measure passed in both the assembly and the legislative council.

From the start, Howe wanted the new Liberal government to rise above petty politics—especially the tradition of patronage appointments—and take the lead in "every noble enterprise." Throughout 1848 and 1849, under Howe's influence, the new government stoutly resisted most attempts to introduce the old principle of "to the victor belong the spoils." The one area where Liberals departed from their principles was in the appointment of magistrates or justices of the peace. On taking office, the Liberals discovered that people who espoused reform attitudes had been systematically excluded as magistrates in most counties and there was an overwhelming predominance of Tories in their ranks. The Liberals' appointment of men who shared their outlook as magistrates elicited howls of disapproval from the Tories, who accused the Liberal government of corruption.

Railways had been Howe's interest for several years, and he believed the government should support their construction. In 1854 he resigned as provincial secretary to accept the appointment of chief commissioner of the Railway Board. Unfortunately, his departure signalled the full return of patronage appointments, this time by the Liberals. It was now the Tories' turn to be disgusted, and James Johnston began to advocate such decidedly un-Conservative measures as universal suffrage, an elected legislative council, and elected municipal institutions.

The Liberals remained in office until 1857, under Uniacke (1848–54) and William Young (1854–57). Meanwhile, Howe was defeated by Dr. Charles Tupper in Cumberland County in 1855, his first electoral loss. Although the Liberals won the election of 1854, they were driven from power by sectarian divisions within the party—Roman Catholics accused Howe and his colleagues of ridiculing Catholic doctrine, leading to a motion of non-confidence and the return of the Conservatives under Johnston in 1857. The religious controversy and Conservative accusations of the extension of the patronage system by the Liberals continued to overshadow assembly proceedings.

In 1859 the so-called Disputed Election took place. Catholic issues had continued to dominate the political agenda in a heated race, which the Liberals won by three seats. The Conservatives tried—unsuccessfully—to have half a dozen elected Liberals disqualified because they held Crown offices. The assembly voted out Conservatives in the session of January 1860 and Howe became provincial secretary in the government of William Young. When Chief Justice Sir Brenton Halliburton died later that year, Young replaced him, and Howe, one of the people most instrumental in the establishment of responsible government in Nova Scotia, finally became premier. Unfortunately, he accomplished little during his term.

During his premiership, Howe operated with a bare majority and he now found the proceedings of the assembly exasperating and exhausting, if not ineffectual. The Conservatives, especially their leader, Tupper, subjected him to continuous attacks in the assembly and in the Tory press. The American Civil War, which started in 1862, put the province's finances in disarray. The war impacted trade and caused a decrease in customs revenues. At the same time, expenditures on the militia increased due to the security situation. Howe's solution was increased taxation—never a popular course of action. Then, during the final year of

Delegates at the Charlottetown Conference, 1864

his government, Howe accepted an imperial appointment as a fisheries commissioner while on a visit to Britain to try to drum up support for the Intercolonial Railway. Once it became known that he would no longer head the government after the next election—no matter what the outcome—Howe was, in modern terms, a "lame-duck" premier.

In the election of 1863, Howe and his government went down in an overwhelming defeat—forty to fourteen—at the hands of the Conservatives, ostensibly led by Johnston but with Tupper actually in charge because of the former's poor health. Due to the magnitude of their loss, the Liberals turned over the reins of government immediately instead of waiting for the next session, introducing a process that continues today. Johnston became premier, to be replaced by Tupper the next year.

Maritime Union

Although the idea of a political union of Britain's North American colonies had been raised occasionally during the early 1860s, it rarely got more serious treatment than as the subject of after-dinner speeches. In the Maritimes, the British Colonial Office supported a union of the three colonies of Nova Scotia, New Brunswick, and Prince Edward Island. Although Maritimers were lukewarm to the idea, they did decide to have a conference to discuss union. But no one took any steps to actually organize the conference. It was only when representatives from the Province of Canada asked to attend that the Maritimers realized they had better organize something—the Charlottetown Conference of August 1864.

Tupper appointed delegates to the conference to consider such a possibility, one that he personally supported. Although Howe did not attend, the Liberals who went in his place became enthusiastic supporters—"Confederates"—of the idea. Delegates from Canada pushed aside the idea of Maritime union for a greater union of all the North American colonies. At the Quebec Conference a month later, proposals for a federation were detailed in seventy-two resolutions, which formed the basis of the British North America Act. The idea of a union of all of Britain's North American colonies was now on the table. But there was little support for the concept in Nova Scotia—where sixty-five percent of the population opposed it—and in Prince Edward Island.

Howe strenuously opposed union, along with several merchants who feared the effect it would have on their businesses. In November 1864 most Nova Scotians joined a grassroots movement against the idea of what the Canadians were calling "Confederation." They could not understand how a central government far inland could even presume to dictate policy to the coastal colonies. To many, some form of union with America was preferred.

Confederation

The British government backed Confederation, seeing colonial union as a way of reducing expenses and commitments, particularly military ones. In fact, one of the major reasons for the creation of Canada was fear of an invasion from the United States. During the Civil War, the British government rushed military reinforcements to North America during several emergencies. British politicians and colonial administrators became dissatisfied with footing the bill for these troop movements—despite the fact that their actions were usually the root cause.

The British believed their best defence against the United States was a federation of their North American colonies, and the colonial secretary directed his colonial governors to support Confederation. In

Lieutenant General Sir William Fenwick Williams, who became lieutenant-governor and was given instructions to ensure Nova Scotia entered Confederation

Nova Scotia, Lieutenant-Governor Sir Richard Graves MacDonnell was removed from his post because he didn't back Confederation. In his place, the British sent out a war hero who was the first Nova Scotian to hold the appointment.

Lieutenant General Sir William Fenwick Williams was born in Annapolis Royal and joined the British Army. During the Crimean War he held the great Turkish fortress of Kars in the Caucasus against the Russians for five months—long enough to scupper a planned Russian advance. Williams was hailed as "The Hero of Kars," knighted, and made a baronet. In November 1865, Williams returned to his home province as lieutenant-governor, with orders to ensure Nova Scotia's support for Confederation.

The next year, a group of Irish Americans who had formed the Fenian Brotherhood in 1857 gave Confederation a much-needed boost. The Fenians' aim was to occupy British North America and hold it hostage, hoping to force England to grant Irish independence. In early 1866, the Fenians prepared to invade British territory in a series of cross-border raids. Some gathered at Eastport, Maine, to occupy New Brunswick's Campobello Island. In response, Williams called out Nova Scotia's sixty-thousand-man militia in March, while the Royal Navy and British army prepared to protect New Brunswick. In April, the attempted incursion collapsed when authorities intercepted coded Fenian telegrams, deciphered them, and arrested the leaders.

The Fenian scare—built up into a bigger threat than it actually was by the advocates of Confederation to gain support for their goal—

was enough to convince many people that union was necessary for their safety. The Nova Scotia assembly, in which a majority had previously been against Confederation, now passed a resolution on April 17 in favour of it, thirty-one to nineteen. The threat of a Fenian invasion had persuaded Nova Scotia politicians to accept Confederation, an unlikely course of events without the Irish-American menace.

In July, Howe and three others went to Britain with instructions from the Anti-Confederation League to demand that the union not occur until the people of Nova Scotia approved it. The trip, anticipated to last four months but which in fact took ten, was to no avail; British Tories and Whigs were both committed to Confederation. Howe was singularly unimpressed with the quality of the debate in both Houses of Parliament on the issue, and was convinced the politicians were quite prepared to let their North American colonies drift into the orbit of the United States.

In the end, the colonies' citizens never got to determine their future; the governments of Nova Scotia—and neighbouring New Brunswick—decided to join the Canadian colonies on July 1, 1867, without putting the question to the electorate (only tiny Prince Edward Island decided against it, at least until 1873).

Joseph Howe was a staunch Anti-Confederate

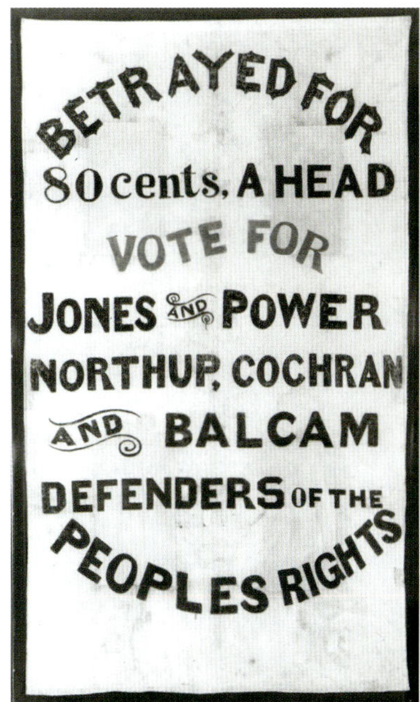

An anti-Confederation banner used in Halifax during the 1867 federal and provincial elections

Sir Charles Tupper, who became prime minister of Canada in 1896

Government After Confederation

Under Confederation, Nova Scotia had fewer responsibilities than it had before. This meant the executive council had to be reorganized, resulting in only four councillors holding office. The attorney general added the duties of the solicitor general to his own, the provincial secretary to those of the financial secretary, the receiver general became the provincial secretary as well, and the commissioner of public works and mines assumed the duties of the Board of Works and the chief commissioner of mines. Although these changes were made without difficulty, another adjustment caused consternation. The assembly was reduced from fifty-five members to thirty-eight, a change that was severely criticized.

Returning to politics—largely because Tupper did not consult the people on their wishes for colonial union—Howe formed an anti-Confederation party and won eighteen of nineteen Nova Scotia seats in the first federal election on September 18, 1867, just eighty days after Confederation came into effect. The lone Confederate seat was won by Tupper, who had entered federal politics. A provincial election took place at the same time, which saw the Anti-Confederates take thirty-six of thirty-eight seats. Clearly, the people of Nova Scotia did not support Confederation.

The effect of this election was enormous and lasted well into the next century. Only a small number of Liberals had supported union, and most Conservatives moved to the Liberals and stayed there. As a result, for the next ninety years the Liberals dominated provincial politics. Anti-Confederation feelings lasted for decades; sixty years later some Nova Scotians still flew flags at half-mast on July 1. In the 1920s, strong anti-Confederation feelings manifested themselves—perhaps for the last time—in a Maritime Rights movement, which objected to the region's diminished influence in the country.

Province House, circa 1871

In February 1868, armed with such clear anti-Confederation support as the provincial and federal elections demonstrated, Howe once again sailed to England to lobby for a repeal of the British North America Act. But British parliamentarians, happy to be rid of the many bothersome problems caused by separate colonies, were not prepared to revisit the issue. Howe returned to Nova Scotia, realizing he had no choice but to make the best of a bad situation. He was able to negotiate better financial terms for the province with Prime Minister Sir John A. Macdonald—who realized belatedly the adverse effect federal duties were having on Nova Scotia's finances—but only on condition that he join the federal cabinet to indicate his unequivocal support for

Sir John A. Macdonald, the first prime minister of a united Canada

Confederation. He did so, becoming president of the Privy Council in 1869, only to be regarded by his supporters and his old political foes as a turncoat.

Howe died four years later, in May 1873, a mere three weeks after being sworn in as his province's lieutenant-governor. On his return to his home province no one had cheered the man who had done more than any other person to bring freedom of the press, freedom of speech, and responsible government to Nova Scotia. One of his biographers noted, "It was the tragedy of his homecoming that killed Howe," while a friend claimed he died "of a broken heart, so deeply wounded by those who had been his friends and should have judged him as stirred by higher motives than anything personal to himself." So bitter were memories of the Confederation issue that it took until 1885 before the legislature granted an annuity of five hundred dollars to Howe's widow, Susan, who only received it for five years before her death.

Over the years, various government acts and bills brought wider democracy to the people. For example, after almost a century, the legislative council of Nova Scotia ceased to exist on May 31, 1928. Most viewed the abolition of this unelected body as long overdue; few bemoaned its demise. Among the most important changes were those that extended the franchise to people who previously had not been allowed to vote or whose interests were not represented.

The members and officers of the Nova Scotia legislative council just prior to the abolition of the council, 1928

Extending the Franchise

On May 20, 1758, the executive council decreed that electors for the first general assembly of Nova Scotia had to be twenty-one years of age, Protestant, and the owner of freehold property worth two pounds. Over time, various restrictions were removed, extending the vote to previously disenfranchised groups. The first of these occurred in 1789, when the religious test (declaration that the Church of England was one's religion) was removed for non-Protestants and Quakers were allowed to forego the oath of allegiance, as all oaths were forbidden by their religion. In 1851, the two-pound freehold property requirement to vote was also eliminated, but voters instead had to pay county or poor rates.

The council continued to remove religious restrictions over the next forty years. In 1826, a bill repealed earlier acts that imposed penalties on Roman Catholics. Four years later this act was clarified to remove any doubts about the entitlement of Catholics to vote and sit in the assembly.

Although a few women in Nova Scotia had voted in the elections of 1793 and 1806, they were not specifically prohibited from voting until the Elective Franchise Act of 1854. That bill established that electors had to be male, at least twenty-one years old, British-born or naturalized, and resident in the province for five years. It specifically excluded "paupers and Indians." In 1870, Nova Scotia introduced the secret ballot, which helped immensely in reducing electoral fraud.

The question of women's suffrage became an issue in the developed world in the last half of the nineteenth century, advocated in many countries, including Canada, by the Women's Christian Temperance Union (WCTU). Women's right to vote was first granted for national elections in New Zealand in 1893 and was followed by several other countries during the next fifty years.

In Canada, women received the franchise during World War One. The controversial Wartime Elections Act of 1917 extended the vote to women in the armed forces and to female relatives of military men. On May 24, 1918, all female citizens aged twenty-one and over became eligible to vote in federal elections, regardless of whether or not they could vote provincially. In July 1919, women attained the right to stand for the House of Commons, although appointment to the Senate was not granted until 1929, after five Alberta women successfully challenged the law prohibiting females from becoming Senators. Throughout the debates that immediately preceded the granting of women's suffrage, the key argument put forth was women's service, sacrifice, and competence during the war. Interestingly, women's service even trumped the argument based on democratic rights.

Provincially, the four western provinces were the first to grant women's suffrage, largely based on their record in helping to settle and build the country. The movement began in Manitoba, where women's suffrage was originally proposed in 1870. The provincial franchise for women was granted in the west during World War One. Manitoba was first, in January 1916, followed by Saskatchewan, Alberta, British Columbia, and Ontario within two years.

In Nova Scotia, the process began in the 1880s, spurred on by the WCTU. Unmarried women who owned property gained the franchise in 1887 for municipal elections. Subsequent bills in 1893 and 1897 to allow women to vote were blocked by Attorney General James Longley. During an 1895 debate in the assembly, he declared that the true functions of women were

> ...first, the bearing and bringing up of children, and this is the highest. Second, the creating of home and beautifying of home life...Third, to charm men and make the world pleasant, sweet and agreeable to live in. Fourth, to be kindly and loving, to be sweet and to be cherished, to be weak and confiding, to be protected and to be the object of man's devotion.

Female property owners attained the provincial franchise and the right to stand for the legislative assembly on April 26, 1918. Two years later the property restriction was removed and universal suffrage finally arrived for everyone over twenty-one. In 1970, the voting age for all was lowered to nineteen, and to eighteen in 1973.

Women first voted in the provincial election of July 1920, and the first females to run in a provincial election were Florence Welton and Louisa Shaw in 1949. Both were defeated. It was 1960 before a female was elected to the assembly, and another twenty-five years before one

Myra Freeman, the first female appointed lieutenant-governor of Nova Scotia

Mayann Francis, the first black person appointed lieutenant-governor of Nova Scotia

became a cabinet minister. In 1981, Alexa McDonough of the New Democratic Party became the first female party leader to sit in a provincial legislature. As of early 2008, only twenty-seven women have been elected as MLAs in Nova Scotia in the forty-eight years since the first was elected.

In 2000, Myra Freeman became Nova Scotia's first female lieutenant-governor. Freeman, who served until 2006, was also the first Jewish vice-regal representative in the province. Her replacement, Mayann Francis, became the second woman and first black person to hold the highest office in Nova Scotia.

Cultural Diversity Representation

In 1992, a report by the Provincial Electoral Boundaries Commission entitled *Effective Political Representation in Nova Scotia* contended that one way to reflect the cul-

First Female MLA

Gladys Porter became the first woman elected to the Nova Scotia legislature. She was born in Sydney in 1894 and received her education locally. In 1914, she married H. Wyman Porter of Kentville and went on to become a councillor for the town (1943–46) and its mayor for two terms (1946–50, 1954–60). Porter was the first female mayor in the Maritimes and resigned to run provincially. She ran for Premier Robert L. Stanfield's Progressive Conservatives in June 1960 and was elected as the member for Kings North, taking her seat on February 8, 1961. She retained her seat in the election of 1963, but did not reoffer for the 1967 election. Porter died ten days after the dissolution of the assembly in April 1967.

Gladys Porter, the first woman elected to the Nova Scotia legislature, 1960

→

The historic occasion when Michaëlle Jean, Canada's first black female governor general, met Mayann Francis, Nova Scotia's first black female lieutenant-governor, February 2007

tural diversity of Nova Scotia was to adopt a broader view of representation in the political process. By establishing constituency boundaries that took these differences into consideration, the interests of the Acadian, black, and Mi'kmaq communities would be protected.

The commission recommended that no changes be made to three ridings with substantial Acadian populations—Clare, Richmond, and Argyle. The Acadians had enjoyed a solid record of representation in the provincial legislature ever since Simon d'Entremont and Frederick Robicheau became the first Acadians elected to the assembly in 1836. Although several Acadians had served in the executive council, the first Acadian cabinet minister with a portfolio was not appointed until 1964.

The Electoral Boundaries Commission also recommended the establishment of the constituency of Preston from the consolidation of black communities in the Preston area. The black population would make up twenty-five to thirty-five percent of this new riding. In the provincial election the next year, three blacks stood as candidates, one of whom was elected.

It was not until 1956 that aboriginals were designated as Canadian citizens. Prior to then, they had no citizenship rights and were considered wards of the Crown. That same year, aboriginals living off reserves were allowed to vote. In 1960 the federal Indian Act of 1876 was amended to permit all registered aboriginal men and women to vote in federal and provincial elections.

Nova Scotia's 1992 Provincial Electoral Boundaries Commission heard submissions from several organizations representing Mi'kmaq communities on its proposal to create a Mi'kmaq seat for the legislature. Although it recommended a new seat representing the province's Mi'kmaq population, it was not established because Mi'kmaq representatives did not present a consolidated, agreed proposal. The House of Assembly Act currently allows First Nation representation in the legislature, upon terms agreed to and approved by the Mi'kmaq people. The issue was later revisited during the commission's ten-year review, but the seat did

FIRST ACADIAN CABINET MINISTER

Gerald Doucet, a barrister, was elected in 1963 as the MLA for the traditionally strong Liberal constituency of Richmond County on Cape Breton Island. He became part of the Progressive Conservative government of Premier Robert L. Stanfield, and continued to serve in the government of Premier George "Ike" Smith when Stanfield jumped to federal politics in 1967. Doucet was appointed to the cabinet on July 6, 1964, becoming the province's first Acadian cabinet minister with a portfolio. At twenty-seven, he was also the youngest cabinet minister in the British Commonwealth.

Doucet held two cabinet posts: provincial secretary (July 1964–December 1967) and minister of education (December 1967–October 1970), and was also minister responsible for civil defence (July 1964–September 1968). He remained an MLA when Premier Gerald Regan's Liberals came to power in 1970. Doucet ran for leadership of the Conservatives in 1971 against John Buchanan and Roland Thornhill, losing to Buchanan on the third ballot. He did not reoffer in the election of 1974.

The Honourable Wayne Adams, the first black Nova Scotian elected to the Nova Scotia legislature, as well as the province's first black cabinet minister, 1993

not materialize. The next opportunity to create the seat will be in 2013. As far as is known, no member of the assembly has declared themselves to be Mi'kmaq, and so there have been no Mi'kmaq members or cabinet ministers.

Over the years, various cabinet ministers have been given responsibilities for certain groups across Nova Scotia, several of whom were formerly disenfranchised, some for a long time. As of early 2008, provincial cabinet ministers have been assigned formal responsibility— through secretariats, offices, or departments—for women (1977), disabled persons (1985), seniors (1989), youths (1989), immigrants (2005), and military relations (2007), as well as for Acadian (1985), aboriginal (1993), African Nova Scotian (2003), and Gaelic affairs (2006).

CONCLUSION
PARTICIPATING IN DEMOCRACY

The Long Struggle for Democracy

WHEN NINETEEN MEMBERS OF THE FIRST elected House of Assembly in Nova Scotia—and in what later became Canada—met for the first time on October 2, 1758, in a humble wooden building at the corner of Argyle and Buckingham streets in Halifax, they had achieved their immediate short-term goal. From then on, the population of the small colony would have a direct voice in the administration of their affairs. No longer would an appointed governor and an appointed executive council alone be responsible for deciding how the province was governed.

Although the achievement was bloodless, it was not painless. Foot-dragging, obfuscation, delaying tactics, misrepresentation, and other means of preventing or prolonging the introduction of an elected assembly had all been employed by a succession of governors and their senior officials. But the people of the colony persisted in their attempts to have an assembly, and in this task they were admirably assisted by the Lords of the Board of Trade and Plantations in Britain. Perversely, men completely detached from the local situation in Nova Scotia—men who lived on the other side of the vast and dangerous North Atlantic Ocean and who had never set foot in the colony—were more interested in furthering the cause of democratic institutions than members of the local establishment.

Undoubtedly, the governors and their comfortable councillors saw the assembly as a threat to their power—a power that was virtually absolute. The Crown appointed the council's members, usually for life, on the advice of the governor from the colony's most powerful and influential people, although in reality its members were selected by the others—the ultimate old boys' club. The members of the council, which functioned like a modern cabinet, headed government departments and provided advice for the governor, who sat at the top of the colonial pyramid.

The councillors not only comprised the colony's ruling elite, they were also its richest members. One way they maintained their wealth was through government patronage and contracts, which they directed to one another in the time-honoured fashion of the old adage, "you scratch my back and I'll scratch yours." The councillors also maintained their positions by favourable intermarriages among their children, nepotism, and the custom of hereditary inheritance of key government posts.

For example, Judge (later Chief Justice) Brenton Halliburton belonged to a council on which his father, two uncles, two brothers-in-law, his father-in-law, son-in-law, aunt's brother-in-law, brother-in-law's father-in-law, and the latter's brother-in-law all held seats at one time or another. Five of them were actually members at the same time.

Even the governors were not above nepotism. When John Wentworth was lieutenant-governor, he got his brother-in-law the position of treasurer in 1793, councillor in 1795, and the offices of secretary, registrar, and clerk of the council in 1796. Wentworth's son, Charles Mary, became a councillor in 1801, and received a recommendation from his father for his uncle's three offices when the latter died in 1808.

Perhaps the most outstanding example of inheritance of government posts was that of the Morris family. Charles Morris became the province's surveyor general on Halifax's founding in 1749 and retained the post for thirty-two years until his death in 1781. In succession, his son (Charles II), grandson (Charles III), and great-grandson (John Spry) inherited the position. Altogether, the Morris family filled the post of surveyor general for its entire century-long existence, from the time it was created until it was merged with the commissioner of crown lands in 1851.

Yet, for the times, such manoeuvring was generally accepted by all, following the lines of the eighteenth-century principle on patronage: that it was not only "a legitimate but an essential instrument of political manipulation." And to be fair to the councillors, the assemblymen themselves were not above seeking tenured offices for themselves or their relatives and friends, or looking after their own personal interests.

When Nova Scotia achieved representative government, the group that was represented was only a small portion of the colony's population. Only white, property-owning, Church of England males over twenty-one years of age could vote or hold office. All five conditions had to be met; anyone who was non-white, non-male, non-Anglican, non-property possessing, or under twenty-one was totally excluded from the democratic process.

Additionally, when representative government—at least to a degree—was attained, it was far from responsible government, where the councillors could be replaced if they no longer held the confidence of a majority in the House of Assembly. In the end, that struggle took much longer to be successful than the attainment of representative government and lasted another ninety years, until 1848. Interestingly, in both battles, it was the governor and the members of the executive council who fought longest and hardest against any change to or diminution of their power.

From these modest beginnings, our system of parliamentary democracy has advanced and grown to the point where the overwhelming majority of citizens can vote and hold elected office, with the only major remaining barrier being age. Sadly, far, far too few people today exercise these hard-won rights. The number of people who vote has been declining for the last half-century, a development that exhibits no sign of stoppage, let alone reversal.

Voter Apathy

One disturbing trend that has vexed politicians over the years is voter apathy. Increased voter turnout imparts greater legitimacy to the victors, which is good for democracy. But fewer and fewer voters are turning out to exercise their franchise in local, municipal, provincial, and federal elections. This downward trend is especially noticeable among young voters, many of whom don't vote once they are old enough to do so. If youths don't vote when they can, the potential exists for them to never cast a vote during their entire adult lives. The net result is that the politicians who get elected are not necessarily the choice of the majority of people, but of the majority who choose to vote.

The statistics are disturbing. In the fourteen Nova Scotia general elections between 1960 and 2006, with only four exceptions, voter turnout has decreased each time from the previous election. From a high of more than eighty-two percent in 1960, it dropped to below sixty percent in 2006, a startling twenty-seven percent decline. Statistics maintained by Elections Nova Scotia highlight this trend:

YEAR	VOTER TURNOUT (%)
1960	82.02
1963	77.87
1967	77.00
1970	77.32
1974	77.89
1978	78.23
1981	74.17
1984	67.52
1988	75.76
1993	75.39
1998	69.47
1999	68.12
2003	65.79
2006	59.89

Table 1. Voter turnout in Nova Scotia general elections, 1960-2006.

In the fifteen federal general elections during the same period, a similar trend occurred. Nationally, the percentage declined from seventy-nine percent in 1962 to less than sixty-five percent in 2006, an eighteen percent decrease. At the provincial level, the decline was from eight-four percent to sixty-four percent, a larger twenty-four percent decrease. Although there are exceptions, Nova Scotian voters have generally turned out in numbers greater than the national average to vote federally.

When comparing the number of Nova Scotians who turn out to vote in provincial elections with the numbers who vote in federal elections, the results are more evenly split. The statistics maintained by Elections Canada do show, however, that in the most recent elections, with a couple of exceptions (including in 2006), fewer Nova Scotians have voted federally than provincially, a reversal of the figures of forty years ago.

YEAR	VOTER TURNOUT CANADA (%)	VOTER TURNOUT NS (%)
1962	79	84
1963	79.2	82
1965	74.8	82
1968	75.7	82
1972	76.7	80
1974	71	74
1979	75.7	75
1980	69.3	72
1984	75.3	75.4
1988	75.3	74.8
1993	70.9	64.7
1997	67	69.4
2000	64.1	62.9
2004	60.9	62.3
2006	64.7	63.9

Table 2. Voter turnout in federal general elections in Canada and Nova Scotia, 1962–2006.

Some countries—such as Australia, perhaps the best-known example—have enacted legislation to try to force people to vote. The Australians believe that certain responsibilities that accompany being a citizen should be enforced, like being required to drive a car on a certain side of the road or turning up to vote. Although it is widely assumed that Australian law requires citizens to vote, strictly speaking that is not the case.

Individuals are required to turn up at a polling station, collect their ballots, enter a booth, and deposit their ballots in a ballot box. Once inside the booth, the individual may choose not to cast any vote, deface the ballot, leave it blank, or even scribble "I'm too stupid to vote" across it. Unfortunately, forcing people to vote—or at least show up at the polling station—is probably not the best way to get them involved in the democratic process.

Disgust with party politics could explain much voter apathy. The low level of decorum in provincial legislatures and the House of Commons, highlighted by such childish behaviour as catcalling, heckling, posturing, grandstanding, lack of attention, and absenteeism, quite simply turns many people against politicians and the political process. Misguided loyalties to party and colleagues before the provincial or national good—even in situations where wrongdoing has occurred—leave people convinced that their representatives are not looking out for the best interests of the electorate but for themselves. Broken or delayed promises add to Canadians' overall dissatisfaction with politicians.

Whatever the reasons—and many have been suggested—declining voter turnout is a sad commentary on the current state of political life provincially and nationally. Few viable solutions have been proposed to resolve the issue. In an attempt to discover its causes in Nova Scotia, in late 2007 the provincial government established a nine-member Select Committee on Participation in the Democratic Process—three from each party—to travel across the province with a remit to investigate the decline and recom-

JOSEPH HOWE ON POLITICIANS

Joseph Howe's opinion of politicians reflects a surprisingly modern view, shared by many today who do not hold our elected representatives in particular high esteem—especially those who believe that politicians continuously place party politics above serving the people. Two quotes from Howe's famous letters to Lord Russell in 1839 illustrate this point. In the first letter he noted, "As a politician, then, your Lordship's only care is, to place or retain your party in the ascendant in the House of Commons." A comment in his second letter is even more pertinent:

> The business of factious demagogues of all parties is to find fault with everything, to propose nothing practical, to oppose whatever is suggested, to misrepresent and to defame. The object of honest and rational politicians ought to be to understand each other—to deal frankly, abhorring concealment, that mistakes may not be made about facts, terms or intentions; to deal fairly, giving credit for a desire to elicit truth and a wish to weigh in a just balance both sides of every question.

mend ways of reversing the trend and other means of participating in democracy.

Canadians have an abundance of freedoms—speech, religion, the press, association, movement, and others. Yet they are choosing not to exercise the one freedom that is the guarantor of all others—the freedom to vote. In particular, the majority of young Canadians aged eighteen to twenty-four are not voting.

Although voting for others to represent Nova Scotians has taken place in the province for 250 years, the freedom to do so has not gone unchallenged. In the twentieth century, Nova Scotian men and women—overwhelmingly young people—crossed the Atlantic and Pacific oceans to fight in two World Wars, the Korean War, and the Cold War. No matter why those wars started, in the final analysis they were fought to ensure our continuing freedoms.

Thousands of Canadians died in those wars; they died for democracy. The best way to honour their sacrifice, to ensure that democracy continues to flourish, is to exercise the most fundamental freedom we have by participating in the political process and exercising our right to vote. There is no more fitting place for this to take place than Nova Scotia, the birthplace of some of the greatest democratic advances in Canada: representative and responsible government, and freedom of the press and freedom of speech. They are unique and unrivalled achievements of which every Nova Scotian should be immensely proud.

APPENDIX 1

CELEBRATING DEMOCRACY

The advent of representative and responsible government in Nova Scotia has been celebrated in the province in many ways over the years. The centennials, sesquicentennials, bicentennials, and sesqui-bicentennials of these key events in the struggle for parliamentary democracy and the people associated with them—especially Joseph Howe—have been honoured by an assortment of postage stamps, medallions, plaques, statues, monuments, buildings, speeches, essays, books, and other means.

REPRESENTATIVE GOVERNMENT

The Dingle Tower

Sir Sandford Fleming (1827–1915) was a Scot-turned-Canadian engineer who was involved in the construction of the Intercolonial Railway and the Canadian Pacific Railway, as well as the laying of the Pacific Cable. He designed Canada's first postage stamp and devised the system of Universal Standard Time. Fleming had a summer home on the Northwest Arm in Halifax and proposed a memorial tower to commemorate the sesquicentennial of representative government in 1908. Through the efforts of the Canadian Club of Halifax, a ten-storey-high tower was erected on the shores of the Northwest Arm opposite peninsular Halifax and Fleming's house, Blenheim Lodge.

Sir Sandford Fleming, who proposed the building of the Dingle Tower to commemorate 150 years of responsible government in 1908

The Dingle Memorial Tower in winter

A 1958 Canadian stamp commemorating the bicentennial of representative government in Nova Scotia

On October 2, 1908, the foundation stone was laid for the tower, which was completed in 1912. The Dingle Tower, named for the old English word for a forest dell, was built in campanile style. Through Fleming's efforts, Canadian provinces and universities, British cities, and the Empire's dominions and colonies contributed the native stone panels that make up the tower. The Dingle Tower stands in thirty-eight hectares of parkland, donated by Fleming on the condition that the tower be built.

Additionally, a memorial tablet was unveiled at Province House in August 1908 by the government of Nova Scotia, listing the members of the first general assembly under representative government. The names of the two members who did not take their seats, Benjamin Gerrish and John Anderson, were not shown.

Bicentennial Celebrations

On the two hundredth anniversary of representative government in 1958, a Committee on the Bicentenary of Representative Government was established to oversee various events. To mark the occasion, provincial archivist C. Bruce Fergusson wrote *The Origin of Representative Government in Canada*, which the committee published. In schools across the province, a bicentenary essay competition took place. Every entrant was given a rectangular bronze medallion bearing the Nova Scotia coat of arms on the obverse (with the shield enamelled in full colour) and an engraving of the Dingle Tower on the reverse. Perhaps the most visible (and useful) sign of the two hundredth anniversary is the Bicentennial Highway, a bypass around the Bedford Highway to get motorists in and out of Halifax quickly.

The Democracy 250 co-chairs, former premiers John Hamm and Russell MacLellan, launch a Democracy 250 licence plate commemorating the sesquibicentennial of representative government

Democracy 250

For the 250th anniversary of representative government in 2008, the government of Nova Scotia passed a bill that established a project team to oversee various initiatives and events marking this significant milestone. In April 2007, former premiers Russell MacLellan and John Hamm were appointed as co-chairs of the Democracy 250 Organizing Committee, made up of representatives from all parties in the legislative assembly and assisted by a small secretariat.

The committee's key objectives were to celebrate history and institutions, educating Canadians about the importance of democracy and voting, honouring veterans and members of the military for upholding our freedoms, and recognizing good citizenship. Throughout 2007, a number of events took place in preparation for the main celebrations in 2008.

In May 2007, a special ceremony was held at Province House to launch the celebrations at which the speaker of the House of Commons, Peter Milliken, gave the keynote address to the legislature. In it, he noted the distressing fact of declining voter turnout in provincial and federal elections. "We must," he said, "instill in our citizens a sense that obligations and duties go hand in hand with the cherished rights that we enjoy as a people."

Democracy 250 hosted a special swearing-in ceremony for 25 new Canadians from 16 countries at Province House on January 30, 2008

A 1948 Canadian stamp commemorating the centennial of responsible government

Other initiatives of Democracy 250 included the launch of a website containing key dates in the evolution of parliamentary democracy in Canada, as well as digital images of important historic documents in the process. On October 2, 2007, the first of seven road signs promoting the anniversary was unveiled on Halifax's Bell Boulevard. The date was chosen deliberately, as it was on that day in 1758 that the first assembly met. In November 2007, an addition to the signs denoting Highway 102 as the Veterans' Memorial Highway proclaimed "They stood firm for democracy." Also in November, commemorative front licence plates featuring the Democracy 250 logo went on sale across the province.

During 2008, events included a special swearing-in ceremony for new Canadians at Province House, discussions with representatives of the Mi'kmaq community about their contribution to the evolution of democracy, a reception in Ottawa on Nova Scotia Day in February, eight youth symposia across the province, a tribute during the Royal Nova Scotia International Tattoo in July, a sunset ceremony on Citadel Hill in August, a public concert on the Grand Parade in September, a conference entitled "Democracy's Shifting Shorelines: Representation, Citizenship and Governance," sponsored by the Atlantic Provinces Political Science Association, and a special session of the legislature on October

2, the actual 250th anniversary of the first session of the first assembly.

RESPONSIBLE GOVERNMENT

The centennial of responsible government in Canada was commemorated in 1948 by a four-cent postage stamp showing busts of Queen Victoria and King George VI—the British monarchs when responsible government began in this country and on its hundredth anniversary, respectively—on either side of the Parliament Buildings in Ottawa. Provincially, a memorial tablet honouring the occasion was unveiled at Province House by the Historic Sites and Monuments Board of Canada. Fifty years later, the sesquicentennial of responsible government in 1998 went largely unremarked by the government, which was criticized by some for this oversight.

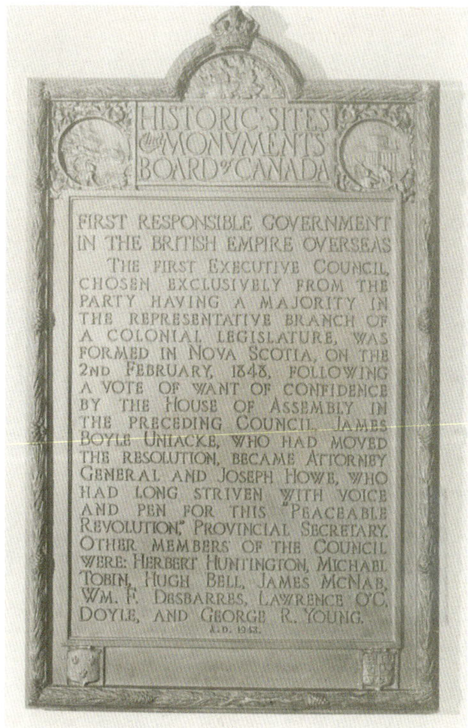

A tablet was erected in Province House in 1948 by the Historic Sites & Monuments Board of Canada commemorating the centennial of responsible government

Joseph Howe

Events honouring responsible government have usually highlighted the key role of Joseph Howe in the process. One of the first instances honouring the advent of responsible government occurred during Queen Victoria's sixtieth anniversary as sovereign in 1897. During celebrations for Diamond Jubilee Week in Halifax, Joseph Howe was hailed as Nova Scotia's greatest statesman, orator, patriot, poet, and journalist. To mark the occasion, the Halifax Cigar Company produced Joe Howe cigars.

A few years later, in 1904, on the hundredth anniversary of Howe's

A 1973 Canadian stamp commemorating the centennial of Joseph Howe's death

birth, a statue of Howe was unveiled on the south grounds of Province House. It faces the harbour, with Howe's arm outstretched towards Britain. The inscription on the statue reads:

JOSEPH HOWE
JOURNALIST, ORATOR, POET, STATESMAN,
PROPHET, PATRIOT, BRITON
BORN AT HALIFAX, DECEMBER 13 1804
"I wish to live and die a British subject; but not a Briton only in name. Give me, give my country the Blessed Privilege of her Constitution and her Laws. Let us be content with nothing less."

Inscriptions on the four corners of the monument read:

JUSTITÆ VINDIX (defender of right)
INTEGER CIVIS (complete citizen)
VIR PROBIS (honest hero)
DICENDI PERITUS (skilled speaker)

Two bronze bas-relief friezes on the monument's north and south sides portray Howe's defence and triumph in his famous libel trial.

In 1969, the Joseph Howe Festival Society was formed and continued into the 1980s. It organized a festival that took place during the fall, in an attempt to attract tourists to the province during the "shoulder" season, outside the prime tourist months. The festival consisted of a costume ball, parade, oratorical contest, craft market, beer fest, and various sporting events.

In 1975, the society first issued a souvenir coin called the Joseph Howe Dollar, which was sold by retail stores, banks, hotels, and restaurants to raise money to finance festival events. The dollar was about the same size and colour as a Canadian silver dollar, with a bust of Howe on one side, and the Halifax city crest on the other. The coins were legal tender in Halifax and Dartmouth from June 30 to October 15 in the year in which they were purchased.

The hundredth anniversary of Howe's death was marked on May 16, 1973, by the issue of an eight-cent postage stamp that displayed a portrait of Howe. Several other features in Halifax honour Howe. Among them are Joseph Howe Drive, Joseph Howe School, the Joseph

This portrait of Joseph Howe hangs beside the Speaker's chair in the legislative assembly

Howe Building, a bust of Howe in another building—Founder's Square—and a plaque on the building that housed his newspaper, the *Novascotian*. In Province House, a 1961 plaque outside the Legislative Library and a small statue inside the library commemorate his historic defence of the libel suit brought against him. A large portrait of Howe also hangs beside the speaker's chair in the legislative assembly.

In 2004, on the two hundredth anniversary of Howe's birth, then Premier John Hamm proclaimed February 2 (the anniversary of the first responsible government) as "Joseph Howe Day." Over the years, there has been an on-again/off-again movement to establish a new provincial statutory holiday in February—usually the third Monday—as a tribute to Howe. Several other provinces have already set up similar

February holidays, with more than half the country's population currently celebrating a long weekend in February.

Howe continues to be a popular subject and over the years numerous books and essays have been published about him, including professor Dr. J. Murray Beck's authoritative two-volume biography, which appeared in 1982–83. On March 20, 2004, essayist and novelist John Ralston Saul (and husband of Governor General Adrienne Clarkson at the time), delivered the inaugural Joseph Howe Lecture at the University of King's College School of Journalism during its Twenty-fifth Anniversary Symposium in Halifax. It was published in 2006 as *Joseph Howe & the Battle for Freedom of Speech*. Since Saul's initial talk, there have been four others: by Nigerian journalist and activist Ken Wiwa, Pulitzer Prize–winning American journalist Tom French, Canadian author Peter C. Newman, and American online war correspondent Kevin Sites. The intention is to stage one lecture each year.

Also in 2004, Trevor J. Adams and Michael Bawtree wrote a book entitled *Today's Joe Howe "the greatest Nova Scotian," 1804-2004, A Birthday Tribute*. The book was published by the Joseph Howe Initiative, an organization established by Bawtree—an actor who often portrays Howe and gives condensed versions of some of his famous speeches—to promote Howe's role and life.

Nova Scotia's Province House symbolizes the beginning of both representative and responsible government in Canada, as well as freedom of speech and freedom of the press

APPENDIX 2

GOVERNORS OF ACADIA, 1603–1710

Acadia changed hands several times during its history, as reflected in the names of its French and British governors. Even while under the control of France, some governors were appointed for separate parts of the colony, while at other times their jurisdictions conflicted with each other.

Pierre du Gua, Sieur de Monts (1603–13)
Jean de Biencourt de Poutrincourt et de Saint-Juste (1606–15)
Charles de Biencourt de Saint-Juste (1615–23)
Sir William Alexander (1621–32)
Charles de Saint-Étienne, Sieur de La Tour (acting) (1624–32)
Isaac de Razilly (1632–35)
Charles de Menou, Sieur d'Aulnay (1635–50)
Charles de Saint-Étienne, Sieur de La Tour (acting) (1635–54)
John Leverett (1654–57)
Sir Thomas Temple (1657–70)
Emmanuel Le Borgne (1657–67)
Alexandre Le Borgne de Bélisle (1667–70)
Héctor d'Andigné de Grandfontaine (1670–73)
Jacques de Chambly (1673–78)
Jurriaen Aernoutsz (Dutch commander) (1674–75)
Cornelis Steenwyck (Dutch governor in name only) (1676–78)
Pierre de Joybert de Soulanges et de Marson (acting) (1677–78)
Michel Leneuf de la Vallière de Beaubassin (acting to 1683) (1678–84)
François-Marie Perrot (1684–87)
Louis-Alexandre des Friches, Sieur de Meneval (1687–90)
Sir William Phips (1690–91)
Joseph Robineau, Sieur de Villebon (1691–1700)
Claude-Sébastien de Villieu (acting) (1700–1701)
Jacques-François Monbeton de Brouillan de Saint-André (acting to 1702) (1701–5)
Simon-Pierre Denys de Bonaventure (1705–6)
Daniel d'Auger, Sieur de Subercase (1706–10)

APPENDIX 3

GOVERNORS, LIEUTENANT-GOVERNORS, AND ADMINISTRATORS OF NOVA SCOTIA, 1710–1786

The early representatives of the British Crown in Nova Scotia held the rank of governor until 1786, during the time of John Parr, when the appointment was downgraded to lieutenant-governor. Early governors sometimes had a lieutenant-governor to assist them, while during periods when there was no vice-regal representative, an administrator was in charge of the affairs of the colony. Such periods without a vice-regal envoy were usually because of a change between governors or a governor's prolonged absence (governors unless otherwise shown).

Annapolis Royal

Colonel Samuel Vetch (Administrator) (1710–11)
Colonel Sir Charles Hobby (Lieutenant-Governor of Annapolis Royal) (1711)
Captain Thomas Caulfeild (Lieutenant-Governor of Annapolis Royal) (1711–17)
Lieutenant General Francis Nicholson (1712–15)
Colonel Samuel Vetch (1715–17)
Colonel (to 1743) & Lieutenant General Richard Phillips (1717–49)
Captain John Doucett (Administrator) (1717–20)
Captain John Doucett (Lieutenant-Governor of Annapolis Royal) (1717–25)
Captain John Doucett (Administrator) (1722–25)
Lieutenant Colonel Lawrence Armstrong (Lieutenant-Governor) (1725–39)
Lieutenant Colonel Alexander Cosby (Lieutenant-Governor of Annapolis Royal) (1739–40)
Major (to 1742) & Lieutenant Colonel Paul Mascarene (Administrator) (1740–49)

Halifax

Colonel Edward Cornwallis (1749–52)
Colonel Peregrine Thomas Hopson (1752–53)
Lieutenant Colonel Charles Lawrence (Administrator) (1753–54)
Lieutenant Colonel Charles Lawrence (Lieutenant-Governor) (1754–56)
Lieutenant Colonel Charles Lawrence (1756–60)
Jonathan Belcher (Administrator) (1760–61)
Henry Ellis (1761–63)
Jonathan Belcher (Lieutenant-Governor) (1761–63)
Lieutenant Colonel Montagu Wilmot (Lieutenant-Governor) (1763–64)

Lieutenant Colonel Montagu Wilmot (1764–66)
Captain William Campbell, Earl Campbell (1766–73)
Benjamin Green (Administrator) (1766)
Michael Francklin (Lieutenant-Governor) (1766)
Michael Francklin (Lieutenant-Governor) (1767–68)
Michael Francklin (Lieutenant-Governor) (1771–72)
Benjamin Green (Administrator) (1771–72)
Michael Francklin (Lieutenant-Governor) (1772)
Lieutenant Colonel Francis Legge (1773–82)
Captain (to 1778) & Rear Admiral Mariot Arbuthnot (Lieutenant-Governor) (1776–78)
Captain Sir Richard Hughes (Lieutenant-Governor) (1778–81)
Commodore Sir Andrew Snape Hamond (Lieutenant-Governor) (1781–82)
Lieutenant Colonel John Parr (1782–86)
Lieutenant Colonel Edmund Fanning (Lieutenant-Governor) (1783–86)

APPENDIX 4

GOVERNORS OF ÎLE ROYALE, 1654–1763, AND LIEUTENANT-GOVERNORS AND ADMINISTRATORS OF CAPE BRETON, 1784–1820

When France ceded Acadia to Britain by the Treaty of Utrecht in 1713, it retained Île Royale (Cape Breton Island) among other locations. The island was under British control between 1745 and 1749 and after 1758.

Nicolas Denys (1654–88)
Joseph Montebon de Brouillan de Saint-Ovide (1713–14)
Philippe Pastour, Sieur de Costebelle (1714–17)
Joseph de Monbeton de Brouillan de Saint-Ovide (acting to 1718) (1717–39)
François Le Coutre de Bourville (acting) (1722–23, 1729–31, 1737–39, 1740)
Isaac-Louis de Forant (1739–40)
Jean-Baptiste-Louis Le Prévost Duquesnel (1740–44)
Louis du Pont Duchambon (acting) (1744–45)
Rear Admiral Sir Peter Warren (1745–46)
Commodore Charles Knowles (1746–47)
Lieutenant Colonel Peregrine Thomas Hopson (acting) (1747–49)
Charles Des Herbiers de la Ralière (1749–51)
Jean-Louis de Raymond, Comte de Raymond (1751–53)
Charles Joseph d'Ailleboust (acting) (1753–54)
Augustin de Boschenry, Chevalier de Drucour (1754–58)
Brigadier (to 1761) & Major General Edward Whitmore (1758–63)

Between 1763 and the arrival of the Loyalists in 1784, Cape Breton Island was ruled from Halifax by the governors of Nova Scotia. In 1784, it became a separate colony with its own government until 1820, when it rejoined Nova Scotia (lieutenant-governors unless otherwise shown).

Joseph Frederick Wallet DesBarres (1784–87)
William Macormick (1787–95)
David Mathews (Administrator) (1795–98)
James Ogilvie (Administrator) (1798–99)
John Murray (Administrator) (1799–1800)
John Despard (Administrator) (1800–1807)
Nicholas Nepean (Administrator) (1807–13)
Hugh Swayne (Administrator) (1813–16)
Jonas Fitzherbert (Administrator) (1816)
George Robert Ainslie (1816–20)
David Stewart (Administrator) (1820)

APPENDIX 5

LIEUTENANT-GOVERNORS AND ADMINISTRATORS OF NOVA SCOTIA, 1786–2008

Beginning with John Parr, the senior vice-regal representative in Nova Scotia held the appointment of lieutenant-governor. Administrators continued to run the affairs of the colony during the lieutenant-governor's absence. The appointment was not used after Confederation (lieutenant-governors unless otherwise shown).

Lieutenant Colonel John Parr (1786–91)
Brigadier General Richard Bulkeley (Administrator) (1791–92)
Sir John Wentworth (1792–1808)
Lieutenant General Sir George Prevost (1808–11)
Alexander Croke (Administrator) (1808–9)
Lieutenant General Sir John Coape Sherbrooke (1811–16)
Duncan Darroch (Administrator) (1814)
Major General George Stracey Smyth (Administrator) (1816)
Lieutenant General George Ramsay, Earl of Dalhousie (1816–20)
Michael Wallace (Administrator) (1818)
Major General (to 1825) & Lieutenant General Sir James Kempt (1820–28)
Michael Wallace (Administrator) (1824–25)
Michael Wallace (Administrator) (1828) (twice)
Major General Sir Peregrine Maitland (1828–34)
Michael Wallace (Administrator) (1829–30)
Thomas Nickleson Jeffery (Administrator) (1832–34)
Major General Sir Colin Campbell (1834–40)
Lucius Bentinck Carey, Viscount Falkland (1840–46)
Sir Jeremiah Dickson (Administrator) (1846)
Lieutenant General Sir John Harvey (1846–52)
John Bazalgette (Administrator) (1851)
John Bazalgette (Administrator) (1852)
Colonel Sir John Gaspard Le Marchant (1852–58)
George Augustus Constantine Phipps, Earl of Mulgrave (1858–63)
Major General Charles Hastings Doyle (Administrator) (1863–64)
Sir Richard Graves MacDonnell (1864–65)
Major General Charles Hastings Doyle (Administrator) (1865)
Lieutenant General Sir William Fenwick Williams (1865–67)

Major General (to 1869) and Lieutenant General Sir Charles Hastings Doyle (1867–73)
Joseph Howe (1873)
Sir Adams George Archibald (1873–83)
Matthew Henry Richey (1883–88)
Archibald Woodbury McLelan (1888–90)
Sir Malachy Bowes Daly (1890–1900)
Alfred Gilpin Jones (1900–1906)
Duncan Cameron Fraser (1906–10)
James Drummond McGregor (1910–15)
David MacKeen (1915–16)
MacCallum Grant (1916–25)
James Robson Douglas (1925)
James Cranswick Tory (1925–30)
Frank Stanfield (1930–31)
Walter Harold Covert (1931–37)
Robert Irwin (1937–40)
Frederick Francis Mathers (1940–42)
Henry Ernest Kendall (1942–47)
John Alexander Douglas McCurdy (1947–52)
Allistair Fraser (1952–58)
Major General Edward Chester Plow (1958–63)
Henry Poole MacKeen (1963–68)
Lieutenant Colonel Victor de Bedia Oland (1968–73)
Dr. Clarence L. Gosse (1973–78)
John Elvin Shaffner (1978–84)
Lieutenant Colonel Alan R. Abraham (1984–89)
Lloyd Roseville Crouse (1989–94)
J. James Kinley (1994–2000)
Myra Freeman (2000–2006)
Mayann E. Francis (2006–)

APPENDIX 6

PREMIERS OF NOVA SCOTIA, 1848–2008

The position of premier began with the introduction of responsible government in 1848, although it was generally referred to as "leader of the government" for the first few years. Previously, the governor or lieutenant-governor governed through the executive council, a body appointed for life.

James Boyle Uniacke (1848–54), Reform (Liberal)
William Young (1854–57), Liberal
James William Johnston (1857–60), Conservative
William Young (1860), Liberal
Joseph Howe (1860–63), Liberal
James William Johnston (1863–64), Conservative
Charles Tupper (1864–67), Conservative
Hiriam Blanchard (1867), Confederate (Conservative)
William Annand (1867–75), Anti-Confederate (Liberal)
Philip Cartaret Hill (1875–78), Liberal
Simon Hugh Holmes (1878–82), Conservative
John Sparrow David Thompson (1882), Conservative
William Thomas Pipes (1882–84), Liberal
William Stevens Fielding (1884–96) Liberal
George Henry Murray (1896–1923), Liberal
Ernest Howard Armstrong (1923–25), Liberal
Edgar Nelson Rhodes (1925–30), Conservative
Gordon Sydney Harrington (1930–33), Conservative
Angus L. Macdonald (1933–40), Liberal
Alexander Sterling MacMillan (1940–45), Liberal
Angus L. Macdonald (1945–54), Liberal
Harold Joseph Connolly (1954), Liberal
Henry Davies Hicks (1954–56), Liberal
Robert L. Stanfield (1956–67), Progressive Conservative
George Isaac Smith (1967–70), Progressive Conservative
Gerald A. Regan (1970–78), Liberal
John M. Buchanan (1978–90), Progressive Conservative
Roger Stuart Bacon (1990–91), Progressive Conservative
Donald W. Cameron (1991–93), Progressive Conservative
John P. Savage (1993–97), Liberal
Russell MacLellan (1997–99), Liberal
Dr. John F. Hamm (1999–2006), Progressive Conservative
Rodney MacDonald (2006–) Progressive Conservative

Appendix 7

Speakers of the Nova Scotia Legislative Assembly, 1758–2008

The position of speaker of the legislative assembly began with representative government in 1758, nearly half a century before political parties existed and ninety years before there was a premier. Traditionally, the speaker, who acts as chairman of the assembly, is appointed by the assembly, now usually from the party in power.

Robert Sanderson (1758–59)
William Nesbitt (1759–83)
Henry Denny Denson (1784–85)
Thomas Cochrane (1784–85)
Sampson Salter Blowers (1785–88)
Richard John Uniacke (1789–93)
Thomas Barclay (1793–99)
Richard John Uniacke (1799–1805)
William Cottnam Tonge (1805–6)
Lewis Morris Wilkins (1806–17), Conservative
Simon Bradstreet Robie (1817–24), Conservative
Samuel George William Archibald (1825–40), Reform
Joseph Howe (1841–43), Reform
William Young (1843–54), Reform
Stewart Campbell (1854–61), Liberal
Alexander C. MacDonald (1861–63), Liberal
John C. Wade (1864–67), Conservative
John J. Marshall (1868–70), Conservative
J. C. Troop (1871–74), Liberal
John B. Dickie (1875), Liberal
Mather B. DesBrisay (1875–76), Liberal
I. Newton Mack (1877–78), Liberal
E. T. Mosley (1879–82), Conservative
Angus McGillvray (1883–86), Liberal
Michael J. Power (1887–94), Liberal
Frederick A. Laurence (1895–1901), Liberal
Thomas Robertson (1902), Liberal
Frederick A. Laurence (1903–4), Liberal
Edward M. Farrell (1905–10), Liberal
George E. Faulkner (1910–11), Liberal
James F. Ellis (1912–16), Liberal

Robert Irwin (1917–25), Liberal
Albert Parsons (1926), Conservative
Daniel George McKenzie (1929–33), Conservative
L. C. Gardner (1934–38), Liberal
Moses E. McGarry (1939), Liberal
G. E. Romkey (1940–53), Liberal
J. Smith McIvor (1954–56), Liberal
W. S. K. Jones (1957–60), Progressive Conservative
Harvey A. Veniot (1961–68), Progressive Conservative
Gordon H. Fitzgerald (1969–70), Progressive Conservative
George M. Mitchell (1970–73), Liberal
James L. Connolly (1973–74), Liberal
Vincent MacLean (1974–76), Liberal
George Doucet (1977–78), Liberal
Ronald Russell (1978–80), Progressive Conservative
Arthur R. Donahoe (1981–91), Progressive Conservative
Ronald Russell (1991–93), Progressive Conservative
Paul MacEwan (1993–96), Liberal
Wayne J. Gaudet (1996–97), Liberal
Gerald G. Fogarty (1997–98), Liberal
Ronald Russell (1998–99), Progressive Conservative
Murray K. Scott (1999–2006), Progressive Conservative
Cecil P. Clark (2006–2007), Progressive Conservative
Alfie MacLeod (2007–), Progressive Conservative

BIBLIOGRAPHY

MAGNA CARTA

Hallam, Elizabeth. *The Plantagenet Chronicles*. New York: Crescent, 1995.

Langley, Andrew. *Mediaeval Life*. London: Dorling Kindersley, 1996.

MI'KMAQ

Paul, Daniel N. *We Were Not the Savages: A Micmac Perspective on the Collision of European and Aboriginal Civilizations*. Halifax: Nimbus, 1993.

Prins, Harald E. L. *The Mi'kmaq: Resistance, Accommodation, and Cultural Survival*. Fort Worth: Harcourt Brace, 1996.

Upton, L. F. S. *Micmacs and Colonists: Indian-White Relations in the Maritimes, 1713-1867*. Vancouver: University of British Columbia, 1979.

PORT ROYAL

Dunn, Brenda. *A History of Port Royal/Annapolis Royal 1605-1800*. Halifax: Nimbus, 2004.

Kerr, W. P. *Port-Royal Habitation: The Story of the French and Mi'kmaq at Port-Royal, 1604-1613*. Halifax: Nimbus, 2005.

SIR WILLIAM ALEXANDER

Finnan, Mark. *The First Nova Scotian*. Halifax: Formac, 1997.

ACADIANS

Candow, James E. *The Deportation of the Acadians*. Ottawa: Environment Canada Parks, 1986.

Faragher, John Mack. *A Great and Noble Scheme: The Tragic Story of the Expulsion of the French Acadians from Their American Homeland*. New York: Norton, 2005.

Mahaffie, Charles D. Jr. *A Land of Discord Always: Acadia from Its Beginnings to the Expulsion of Its People 1604-1755*. Camden, Me.: Down East, 1995.

Reid, John G., Maurice Basque, Elizabeth Mancke, Barry Moody, Geoffrey Plank and William Wicken. *The 'Conquest' of Acadia, 1710: Imperial, Colonial, and Aboriginal Constructions*. Toronto: University of Toronto, 2004.

LOUISBOURG

Johnston, A. J. B. *Control and Order in French Colonial Louisbourg, 1713–1758.* East Lansing: Michigan State University, 2001.

McLennan, J. S. *Louisbourg From its Foundation to its Fall, 1713–1758.* Fourth ed. Toronto: Bryant, 1979.

REPRESENTATIVE GOVERNMENT

Fergusson, C. Bruce. *The Origin of Representative Government in Canada.* Halifax: Committee on Bicentenary of Representative Government, 1958.

Reid, Dr. John. "Nova Scotia's Representative Assembly, 1758: A Historical Perspective." http://www.democracy250.ca.

NEW ENGLAND PLANTERS

Candow, James E. *The New England Planters in Nova Scotia.* Ottawa: Environment Canada Parks, 1986.

AMERICAN REVOLUTIONARY WAR

Brebner, John Bartlet. *The Neutral Yankees of Nova Scotia: A Marginal Colony during the Revolutionary Years.* New York: Russell & Russell, 1937.

Clarke, Ernest. *The Siege of Fort Cumberland, 1776: An Episode in the American Revolution.* Montreal & Kingston: McGill-Queen's University Press, 1995.

LOYALISTS

MacKinnon, Neil. *This Unfriendly Soil: The Loyalist Experience in Nova Scotia, 1783–1791.* Kingston and Montreal: McGill-Queen's University Press, 1986.

WAR OF 1812

Boileau, John. *Half-Hearted Enemies: Nova Scotia, New England and the War of 1812.* Halifax: Formac, 2005.

RESPONSIBLE GOVERNMENT

Adams, Trevor J. & Michael Bawtree. *Today's Joe Howe "the greatest Nova Scotian," 1804–2004, A Birthday Tribute.* Halifax: Joseph Howe Initiative, 2004.

Beck, J. Murray. *Joseph Howe, Vol. I, Conservative Reformer 1804–1848.* Kingston & Montreal: McGill-Queen's University Press, 1982.

Langstone, Rosa W. *Responsible Government in Canada*. London & Toronto: Dent, 1931.

Chisholm, Joseph Andrew (ed). *The Speeches and Public Letters of Joseph Howe, Vol. I (1804–1848)*. Halifax: Chronicle, 1909.

Livingston, W. Ross. *Responsible Government in Nova Scotia: A Study of the Constitutional Beginnings of the British Commonwealth*. Iowa City, Iowa: University of Iowa, 1930.

Saul, John Ralston. *Joseph Howe & the Battle for Freedom of Speech*. Kentville, N.S.: Gaspereau, 2006.

Sherwood, Roland H. *Jotham Blanchard The Forgotten Patriot of Pictou*. Hantsport, N.S.: Lancelot, 1982.

GOVERNMENT OF NOVA SCOTIA—GENERAL

Beck, J. Murray. *The Government of Nova Scotia*. Toronto: University of Toronto, 1957.

———. *Politics of Nova Scotia, Vol. I, Nicholson-Fielding 1710–1896*. Tantallon, N.S.: Four East, 1985.

———. *Politics of Nova Scotia, Vol. II, Murray-Buchanan 1896–1988*. Tantallon, N.S.: Four East, 1988.

Cuthbertson, Brian. *Johnny Bluenose at the Polls: Epic Nova Scotian Election Battles 1758–1848*. Halifax: Formac, 1994.

———. "Short History of Elections and Voting in Nova Scotia 1758–2006." http://www.democracy250.ca.

HISTORY OF NOVA SCOTIA—GENERAL

Akins, Thomas B. *The History of Halifax City*. Halifax: Brook House, 2002.

Bruce, Harry. *An Illustrated History of Nova Scotia*. Halifax: Communications Nova Scotia & Nimbus, 1997.

McCreath, Peter L. and John G. Leefe. *A History of Early Nova Scotia*. Tantallon, N.S.: Four East, 1982.

Raddall, Thomas H. *Halifax: Warden of the North*. Halifax: Nimbus, 1993.

IMAGE CREDITS

John Boileau 4, 6, 196B, 198B, 200

Library and Archives Canada 7, 9, 10, 11, 14, 15T, 15B, 16, 19T, 26, 27, 34, 35, 42B, 47, 49, 61, 63, 69, 70, 71, 72, 73, 76, 85, 86, 89T, 90T, 90B, 91, 95, 99, 102T, 105, 108, 119, 120, 121, 129, 136, 137T, 137M, 137B, 138T, 138B, 139, 144, 151, 152, 157, 158, 174, 176, 195

Nova Scotia Archives and Records Management 12, 13T, 13B, 22, 23, 25, 30, 36, 38, 39, 42T, 45, 46, 48, 62, 78, 88, 100, 102B, 104, 107, 110, 122, 131, 140, 149, 153, 154, 159, 160, 163, 167, 172, 177T, 177B, 179T, 179B, 196T, 199

The Province of Nova Scotia 18, 37, 64, 92, 94, 101, 111, 126, 150T, 150B, 161, 178, 183TL, 183TR, 184, 201, 202

New Brunswick Museum 19B

Dalhousie University 80, 82, 89B

Saint Mary's University 87

Private Collection 97, 127

West Pubnico Musée Acadien & Research Centre 132

Province House Collection 180, 183B

Nova Scotia Legislative Library 186

Democracy 250 Organizing Committee 197, 198T

The Nova Scotia coat of arms appearing on the cover and on page 17 is courtesy of the Province of Nova Scotia

Index

A

Abercrombie, General James 70
aboriginal representation in
    government 185
Acadia ix, 14, 15, 18, 19, 23, 24, 25, 26
    first year 12
    founding 11–12
Acadian 47, 48, 51, 54
    deputies under British 29, 40, 49
    Expulsion 43, 49
    as "French Neutrals" 48
    move to Cape Breton 31
    population 25, 29, 46, 50
    refusal to take oath of allegiance
      27, 30, 49
    representation in government 185
    return 77
    way of life 22–23
    See also assembly, first Acadian
      members
Acadian (newspaper) 127
Acadian Recorder (newspaper) 125
Act of Incorporation (Halifax) 130
Act of Union 145
Adams, Trevor J. 202
Adams, Wayne 186
A Great and Noble Scheme 24
Alexander, William x, 15–16, 17
Alexander, William (the Younger) 16
Allan, John 81
Almon, Mather Byles 163, 164, 168
American Civil War 173
American Revolution 36, 66, 77, 78,
    79, 85, 94, 109, 114, 115
Amherst, Major General Jeffrey 70
Amherst (town) 75

Anderson, John 64, 196
Annand, William 131
Annapolis Royal ix, 26, 27, 34, 36, 46,
    56, 59, 75, 176
    See also Port Royal
Arbuthnot, Mariot 85
Argall, Samuel 14
Armstrong, Lawrence 28, 30
assembly 53, 65, 102, 106
    Belcher's proposal 51
    Board of Trade and Plantation's
      direction 60
    Civil List debate 140
    development of 112–13
    disagreements with council of 68
    distrust in 155
    first Acadian members of 132
    first black members of 186
    first by-election of 61
    first election of 60
    first electors and elected of 66
    first female members of 183
    first members of 62–64
    first Roman Catholic member of
      107
    first session of 61
    Halifax domination of 69
    Lawrence's opposition to 52, 54,
      56, 57
    reaction to War of 1812 of 100
    remuneration for members of 112
    settlers' reaction to Lawrence's
      delays of 58–59
    transatlantic debate over 53
Atwell, Yvonne 186